Doctrine and Covenants Stories

Published by
The Church of Jesus Christ of Latter-day Saints
Salt Lake City, Utah

Contents

Maps and Chart

Sources

Some of the information in this book is taken from the nonscriptural sources cited below for each chapter.

Key to abbreviations:

DDC Smith, Hyrum M. , and Sjodahl, Janne M. *Doctrine and Covenants Commentary*. Rev. ed. Salt Lake City: Deseret Book Co. , 1972.

ECH Smith, Joseph Fielding. *Essentials in Church History*. Classics in Mormon History Series. Salt Lake City: Deseret Book Co. , 1979.

HC Smith, Joseph. *History of The Church of Jesus Christ of Latter-day Saints*. 7 vols. 2d ed. rev. Edited by B. H. Roberts. Salt Lake City: The Church of Jesus Christ of Latter-day Saints, 1932–51.

HJS Smith, Lucy Mack. *History of Joseph Smith*. 1945. Reprint. Salt Lake City: Bookcraft, 1954.

HRS Relief Society. *History of Relief Society, 1842–1966*. Salt Lake City: General Board of Relief Society, 1967.

MD McConkie, Bruce R. *Mormon Doctrine*. 2d ed. Salt Lake City: Bookcraft, 1966.

Chapter 1: ECH, chapter 6; HJS, p. 341.
Chapter 4: ECH, chapter 9.
Chapter 5: ECH, chapter 9.
Chapter 6: ECH, chapter 9.
Chapter 7: ECH, chapter 10.
Chapter 9: ECH, chapter 12.
Chapter 11: ECH, chapter 13.
Chapter 12: ECH, chapter 13.
Chapter 14: ECH, chapter 14.
Chapter 15: ECH, chapter 14.
Chapter 16: ECH, chapter 14.
Chapter 17: ECH, chapter 15.
Chapter 21: ECH, chapter 15.
Chapter 22: HC, vol. 1, chapter 15; ECH, chapter 15.
Chapter 23: ECH, chapter 17.
Chapter 25: ECH, chapter 17.
Chapter 27: ECH, chapter 17.
Chapter 28: ECH, chapter 17; HC, Vol. 1, chapter 19.
Chapter 29: ECH, chapter 18.
Chapter 30: ECH, chapter 16; HC, vol. 1, chapter 22.
Chapter 31: ECH, chapter 18; DCC, section 89.
Chapter 32: ECH, chapter 18, 20.
Chapter 34: ECH, chapter 19.
Chapter 35: ECH, chapter 19.
Chapter 36: ECH, chapter 20.
Chapter 37: ECH, chapter 21; MD, "Deacons. "
Chapter 38: ECH, chapters 13, 21, 30.
Chapter 39: ECH, chapter 21.
Chapter 41: ECH, chapter 22.
Chapter 42: ECH, chapter 23.
Chapter 45: ECH, chapters 24, 25, 26.
Chapter 46: ECH, chapter 26.
Chapter 47: ECH, chapters 25–26.
Chapter 48: ECH, chapters 22, 28.
Chapter 50: ECH, chapter 30.
Chapter 51: HRS, pp. 18–25.
Chapter 52: ECH, chapter 31.
Chapter 53: HC, vol. 5, p. 267.
Chapter 54: ECH, chapter 32.
Chapter 55: ECH, chapter 34
Chapter 56: ECH, chapter 35.
Chapter 57: ECH, chapter 36.
Chapter 58: ECH, chapters 36, 37.
Chapter 59: ECH, chapters 36, 37.
Chapter 60: ECH, chapter 37.
Chapter 61: ECH, chapter 38.
Chapter 62: ECH, chapters 37, 39.
Chapter 63: ECH, chapters 40–43.

Before the Doctrine and Covenants

We lived in heaven before we came to earth. Our Heavenly Father gave us the plan of salvation. The plan of salvation helps us get ready to live in heaven again. If we obey the plan, we can live with Heavenly Father after we are resurrected.

Jesus lived with us in heaven. He wanted to obey Heavenly Father's plan. Jesus said he would come to earth and be our Savior. He would do Heavenly Father's work.

Satan lived with us in heaven too. But he was wicked. He would not obey Heavenly Father's plan. Heavenly Father made Satan leave heaven. Satan wants to destroy the plan of salvation. He wants to stop Heavenly Father's work.

Jesus made the earth. Heavenly Father's children came to live on it. Jesus sent prophets to teach them to be righteous. Some of the people obeyed the prophets.

Other people on earth would not listen to the prophets. These people obeyed Satan. They became wicked.

The Old Testament tells about people who lived in Palestine long ago. Those people knew about Jesus. Righteous people had his gospel. Righteous men had the priesthood. Prophets taught the people that Jesus would come to earth. He would be their Savior.

The Book of Mormon tells about people who lived in America long ago. They knew about Jesus. They had his gospel. Righteous men had the priesthood. Prophets taught the people in America that Jesus would be their Savior. He would visit them after he was resurrected.

Jesus Christ came to live on earth. The New Testament tells about his life on earth. Jesus taught people his gospel. He taught them to obey Heavenly Father's commandments.

Jesus chose twelve men to be Apostles. He gave them the priesthood. He started his church. Many people loved Jesus. They were righteous and obeyed his teachings.

Satan did not want people to obey Jesus. Satan tempted people, and they became wicked. They would not believe in Jesus. They hated Jesus. They killed him.

After three days, Jesus was resurrected. He talked with his Apostles. He told them to teach the gospel to all people. Jesus also visited the righteous people in America. Then he went to heaven to be with his Father.

The Apostles were the leaders of the Church of Jesus Christ. They went to many lands. They taught people the gospel. Many people believed in Jesus and were baptized. The Apostles gave righteous men the priesthood. There were many members of the true Church of Jesus Christ.

Satan wanted to destroy the Church of Jesus Christ. He tempted people, and they obeyed him. Many people stopped believing in Jesus. The wicked people killed the righteous members of the Church. They killed the Apostles. There were no leaders for the Church. There was no one on earth to give the priesthood to men.

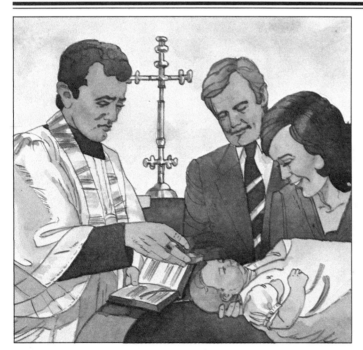

Some people changed the teachings of the Church of Jesus Christ. They changed the commandments of God. The true church that Jesus had started was gone. People started churches of their own. But none of the churches was the true church.

Hundreds of years went by. There were many different churches on earth. But none of them was the true Church of Jesus Christ. The members of the churches believed in Jesus Christ. But the churches did not have the true gospel. They did not have the priesthood of God. They did not have prophets or Apostles.

Jesus said he would come to earth again. He said his true church must be on the earth before he comes again. People must know his true gospel. Men must have the priesthood. There must be prophets and Apostles. There must be revelations.

Revelations come from Jesus. Revelations tell us things Jesus wants us to know. They tell us what he wants us to do. Jesus gives revelations to his prophets. The revelations are for his true church.

The Doctrine and Covenants is a book of revelations. The Doctrine and Covenants tells about the true Church of Jesus Christ. It tells about the priesthood. It tells about prophets and Apostles. The Doctrine and Covenants tells what we must do to be ready when Jesus comes again.

The book you are reading is about the Doctrine and Covenants. This book tells about some of the revelations. It tells how the true Church of Jesus Christ was brought back to the earth. It also tells about some of the people who lived when the Church was started.

Joseph Smith and His Family

Chapter 1 (1805–1820)

Joseph Smith was born 23 December 1805. His family lived in the state of Vermont. Vermont is in the United States of America. Joseph Smith's father was named Joseph, too. His mother's name was Lucy.

Joseph Smith—History, 1:3–4

Joseph had six brothers and three sisters. One baby brother died.

Joseph Smith—History, 1:4

Joseph's father and mother were good people. They loved their children. They worked hard to take care of their children.

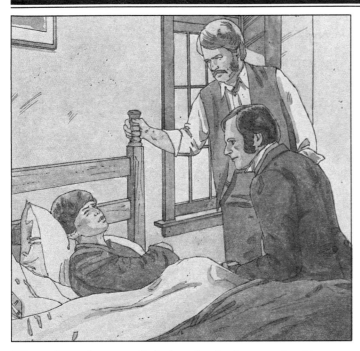

When Joseph was a little boy he had a very bad sore on his leg. Doctors tried to make his leg better, but they could not.

Hyrum Smith was Joseph's older brother. He loved Joseph. Hyrum was sorry Joseph's leg hurt so much. He sat by Joseph's bed. He tried to help Joseph feel better.

The doctors wanted to cut off Joseph's leg. His mother would not let them. So they decided to cut out part of the bone. Joseph knew his leg would hurt when the doctors cut it. But he had faith. He knew Heavenly Father would help him.

The doctors asked Joseph to drink some wine so the pain would not be so bad. Joseph would not drink the wine. Joseph asked his mother to go outside. He did not want her to see the doctors cut into his leg.

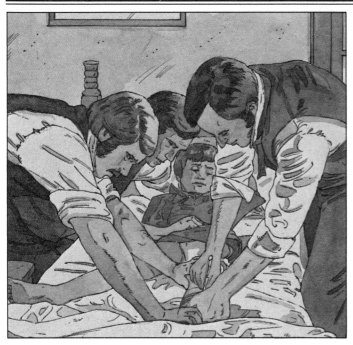

Joseph asked his father to hold him. The doctors cut into Joseph's leg. They cut out the bad parts of the bone. This hurt Joseph very much. But he was very brave. After many days his leg was better.

When Joseph was older, his family moved to the state of New York. They lived in a log house on a farm near Palmyra.

Joseph Smith—History, 1:3

Joseph's family was poor. They had to work hard to pay for the farm. The boys helped their father plant crops. They took care of the animals. The girls worked with their mother.

Joseph Smith—History 1:46

Joseph was a good boy. He was happy. He liked to laugh and have fun.

Joseph Smith—History 1:28

Joseph Smith's First Vision

Chapter 2 (1820)

Joseph Smith and his family believed in God. They read the Bible together. Joseph's father and mother taught their children to be good.

There were many churches in Palmyra. All the people said their church was the right church. They said the other churches were wrong. Joseph did not know which church to join. He wanted to know which was the true Church of Jesus Christ.

Joseph Smith—History 1:5–10

One day Joseph was reading the Bible. He was fourteen years old. He read that we should ask God when we want to know something. Joseph decided to pray. He would ask God which church to join.

Joseph Smith—History 1:11–13; James 1:5

It was a beautiful spring day. Joseph went to the woods near his home.
He knelt down. He prayed out loud. He had faith that Heavenly Father
would answer his prayer.

Joseph Smith—History 1:14–15

Satan did not want Joseph to pray. Satan tried to stop
him. Satan made it dark all around Joseph. He could
not talk. He was afraid.

Joseph Smith—History 1:15

Joseph did not stop praying. Satan could not make
him stop.

Joseph Smith—History 1:16

Then Joseph had a vision. He saw a beautiful, bright light. The light was all around him. He saw Heavenly Father and Jesus Christ. They were standing above him in the light. Heavenly Father pointed to Jesus Christ and said, "This is my Beloved Son. Hear him!"

Joseph Smith—History 1:16–17

Joseph asked Jesus which church was true. He asked which church he should join. Jesus told Joseph not to join any of the churches. Jesus said all the churches were wrong. None of them was his church. He told Joseph many other things. Then the vision ended. Joseph was alone.

Joseph Smith—History 1:18–20

Joseph went home. His mother asked if he was all right. Joseph said yes. He told his mother he saw a vision. He told her what he learned in his vision.

Joseph Smith—History 1:20

Joseph told some people in the town about his vision. The people did not believe him. They thought he was telling a lie. They were angry at him. They were mean to him.

Joseph Smith—History 1:21–23

Joseph always told the truth about his vision. He knew he had seen Heavenly Father and Jesus Christ. He knew that none of the churches on earth was true.

Joseph Smith—History 1:25–26

The Angel Moroni and the Gold Plates

Chapter 3 (1823–1827)

Three years went by after Joseph's first vision. He was seventeen years old. Joseph wondered what God wanted him to do. One night Joseph prayed. He had faith that God would tell him what to do.

Joseph Smith—History 1:27, 29

Joseph saw a bright light in his room. An angel was standing in the light. The angel's face was very bright. He wore a beautiful white robe.

Joseph Smith—History 1:30–32

The angel said his name was Moroni. God had sent him to talk to Joseph. Moroni said God had a work for Joseph to do.

Joseph Smith—History 1:33

The Angel Moroni told Joseph about a book. The book was about the people in America long ago. Jesus Christ came to these people. He taught them his gospel.

Joseph Smith—History 1:34

Moroni said the book was written on gold pages. The gold pages were called plates. The book was written in a language we do not know. God wanted Joseph to translate the book. Joseph would write it in words we know.

Joseph Smith—History 1:34–35

The Angel Moroni said the plates were hidden in a hill near Joseph's home. They were buried in the ground. Moroni said two stones were hidden with the gold plates. The stones were called the Urim and Thummim. The stones would help Joseph translate the book.

Joseph Smith—History 1:34–35, 42, 51

Moroni told Joseph about Elijah. Elijah was a great prophet who lived long ago. Elijah had the priesthood. The story of Elijah is in the Old Testament. Moroni said Elijah would come back to earth. Elijah would tell people to learn about their ancestors. Ancestors are members of our family who lived before us.

Joseph Smith—History 1:38–39; D&C 2:1–2

Moroni told Joseph about the priesthood. The priesthood is the power of God. Moroni said Elijah would bring priesthood power to the earth. The priesthood power would help righteous families. They could be sealed. Then they could live together forever. Moroni went away.

Joseph Smith—History 1:38–39, 40; D&C 2:1–2

The Angel Moroni came back two more times that night. He told Joseph many things each time. He left when it was morning. Joseph got up and went to work with his father on the farm.

Joseph Smith—History 1:43–49

Joseph was too tired to work. He fell down. While he was lying down, Moroni came again. Joseph told his father the things Moroni taught him. Joseph's father believed him. He knew God had sent Moroni. He told Joseph to obey Moroni.

Joseph Smith—History 2:48, 50

Joseph went to find the gold plates. He went to a hill near his home. It was the Hill Cumorah. The gold plates were there. They were buried under a big rock. They were in a stone box. The Urim and Thummim were also in the box.

Joseph Smith—History 1:51–52

The Angel Moroni came to Joseph. He would not let Joseph take the gold plates home. He told Joseph to come to the hill on the same day each year for four years.

Joseph Smith—History 1:53

Joseph obeyed Moroni. He went to the Hill Cumorah each year. Moroni taught him there. Moroni told Joseph about the true Church of Jesus Christ. Jesus would start his church on the earth again.

Joseph Smith—History 1:54

In 1827, Moroni gave the gold plates to Joseph. Joseph had waited four years to get the plates. Moroni told Joseph to take good care of the plates.

Joseph Smith—1:59

Joseph took the gold plates home. He wanted to take good care of them. Wicked men tried to steal them. Joseph hid the gold plates where the wicked men could not find them. God helped Joseph keep the gold plates safe.

Joseph Smith—1:60

Martin Harris and the Lost Pages

Chapter 4 (1824–1828)

Joseph Smith's family was poor. They needed money. Joseph wanted to help his family. He went to the state of Pennsylvania to work. He lived with a man named Mr. Hale.

Joseph Smith—1:56–57

Mr. Hale had a daughter named Emma. Joseph met Emma. They fell in love and got married. They went to live with Joseph's family. Joseph helped his father work on the farm.

Joseph Smith—History 1:57–58

Many people knew Joseph had the gold plates. They tried to steal them. The people made trouble for Joseph. They told lies about Joseph and his family.

Joseph Smith—History 1:60–61

The trouble was so bad that Joseph and Emma decided to move. They wanted to go to Pennsylvania. They would live near Emma's family. But Joseph and Emma did not have enough money to go.

Joseph Smith—History 1:61

A man named Martin Harris lived near Joseph Smith. Martin Harris had a big farm. He had a lot of money. Martin Harris was kind to Joseph and Emma. He gave them money to help them move. Joseph and Emma went to Pennsylvania.

Joseph Smith—History 1:61–62

Joseph began to translate the writing on the gold plates. Joseph did not know what the writing meant. God helped him. Joseph used the Urim and Thummim to understand the words. We can read what he translated. It is called the Book of Mormon.

Joseph Smith—History 1:62

Martin Harris went to Pennsylvania. He helped Joseph translate. Joseph read the words from the gold plates. Martin wrote them on paper. Joseph and Martin translated 116 pages of the Book of Mormon.

Martin Harris wanted to take the 116 pages home. He wanted his family to see them. Joseph asked the Lord if Martin could take the pages home. The Lord said no. Joseph asked again. The Lord said no again.

Martin still wanted to take the pages home. Joseph asked again. This time the Lord said Martin could take the pages home. The Lord said Martin could show the pages to his family. But he must not show them to other people.

Martin promised to obey the Lord. He took the pages home. He showed them to his family. But he did not keep his promise. He showed the pages to some other people. Then he put the pages away.

Later Martin went to get the pages. He looked everywhere. He could not find them. The pages were lost.

Joseph was very worried about the lost pages. He could not sleep.

Jesus talked to Joseph. He said Martin Harris had done a wicked thing. Martin promised to obey the Lord. But he did not keep his promise. Now the pages of the Book of Mormon were lost. Martin Harris could not help translate again.

D&C 3:12–14

Jesus said Satan wanted the 116 pages to be lost. Wicked men had the pages. Satan and the wicked men wanted to stop God's work. They did not want people to believe the Book of Mormon. Jesus said Satan could not stop God's work. Wicked men could not stop God's work.

D&C 10: Preface, 8, 12, 22–29, 33, 43

Jesus told Joseph not to worry about the stories that were on the lost pages. The same stories were written in another part of the gold plates. Jesus said Joseph should translate the other part of the plates. Then good people could read the Book of Mormon. They would believe the book was true. They would learn the gospel.

D&C 10:30, 41, 52, 62–63

Joseph Smith and Oliver Cowdery

Chapter 5 (February–April 1829)

Joseph and Emma Smith lived on a little farm near Harmony, Pennsylvania. Joseph's father came to visit them. They were happy to see him. Joseph's father was a good man.

Jesus gave Joseph a revelation for his father. The revelation told how people could help Jesus. They should love Jesus. They should work hard to teach the gospel. They should love and help other people.

D&C 4:2–6

People who want to be missionaries and help Jesus should study and learn. They should have faith. They should pray. Jesus said people who help him will be blessed.

D&C 4:5–7

Joseph's father went home. He tried to do the things Jesus told him to do.

Joseph had to work on his farm. He also needed to translate the gold plates. He had too much work to do. Joseph prayed and asked God for help.

God answered his prayer. God sent a man named Oliver Cowdery to Joseph. Oliver Cowdery wanted to know about the gold plates. Joseph told Oliver about Moroni and the plates. He told Oliver about the Book of Mormon.

Oliver believed Joseph. Oliver said he would help Joseph translate the gold plates. Joseph read the words out loud. Oliver wrote the words on paper. Joseph and Oliver worked hard.

Jesus taught Joseph and Oliver many things. He said they should not try to be rich. They should learn about God. He said they should help people learn the gospel. Jesus said they should have faith and do good things. If they did, they could live with Heavenly Father forever.

D&C 6:7, 8, 11, 13

Jesus said Oliver should always be Joseph's friend. He should always help Joseph. Jesus said Oliver could learn to translate like Joseph. The Holy Ghost would help Oliver read the words of the Book of Mormon, but Oliver must have faith. And he must think hard about the words.

D&C 6:18, 25; 8:1–2

Oliver tried to translate. He thought it would be easy. He did not think about the words. He wanted God to tell him the words. He could not translate.

D&C 9:1, 5, 7

Oliver did not try to translate the Book of Mormon again. Joseph translated the plates. Oliver wrote the words for Joseph. Jesus said Oliver should work hard when he helped Joseph. Then Jesus would bless Oliver.

D&C 9:14

Jesus said Oliver had not asked for God's help in the right way. Jesus told Joseph Smith how Oliver and all people can get help from God.

D&C 9:7

When people need help they should think about what to do. They should decide what is right.

D&C 9:8

Then they should ask God if it is right. If it is right, they will feel good in their hearts. They will know it is right.

D&C 9:8

If it is wrong, they will not feel good in their hearts.

D&C 9:9

Joseph and Oliver Are Given the Priesthood

Chapter 6 (May 1829)

Joseph Smith and Oliver Cowdery were translating the Book of Mormon. They read about baptism. They wanted to know more about baptism.

Joseph Smith—History 1:68

Joseph and Oliver decided to ask God. They had faith God would help them learn the truth. On 15 May 1829, they went into the woods and prayed.

Joseph Smith—1:68, 72

An angel came to Joseph and Oliver. A bright light was all around the angel. The angel was John the Baptist. He baptized Jesus long ago.

Joseph Smith—History 1:68, 72

John the Baptist had come to give Joseph and Oliver the priesthood.
The priesthood is the power of God. He gave Joseph and Oliver the
Aaronic Priesthood. Priests in the Aaronic Priesthood have
power to baptize people.

D&C 13; Joseph Smith—History 1:68-69

John the Baptist told Joseph and Oliver to baptize each other. Joseph baptized Oliver. Then Oliver baptized Joseph. They went down under the water when they were baptized.

Joseph Smith—History 1:70-71, 73

Long ago John the Baptist had baptized Jesus the same way. Jesus went down under the water when he was baptized.

Matthew 3:16

Joseph and Oliver were filled with the Holy Ghost after they were baptized. The Holy Ghost told them the true Church of Jesus Christ would soon be on the earth again.

Joseph Smith—History 1:73

Joseph and Oliver told their good friends they had been baptized. They told them about the priesthood. But Joseph and Oliver did not tell other people. They knew wicked people would not believe them. Wicked people would make trouble for them.

Joseph Smith—History 1:74–75

A few days later, three other angels came. They were Peter, James, and John. They were Apostles of Jesus long ago. Peter, James, and John gave Joseph Smith and Oliver Cowdery the Melchizedek Priesthood.

D&C 27:12

The priesthood of God was on the earth again. Now righteous men
could have priesthood power. Men who have the Melchizedek Priesthood
can be Church leaders. They can bless people. They can give people the
gift of the Holy Ghost.

D&C 20:41–44

Witnesses See the Gold Plates

Chapter 7 (1829–1830)

Joseph Smith and Oliver Cowdery finished translating the Book of Mormon. Jesus Christ wanted people to read the Book of Mormon. He wanted them to know Joseph told the truth about the gold plates. Jesus wanted people to know the gold plates were real.

D&C 17:4–5

Joseph Smith was the only person who had seen the gold plates. Jesus chose three other men to see the gold plates. The men were called witnesses. The men were Martin Harris, Oliver Cowdery, and David Whitmer.

D&C 17:1

Joseph took the three witnesses into the woods. They prayed. An angel came and showed them the gold plates. He showed them the writing on the plates. Jesus told the three witnesses to write about the things they saw.

D&C 17:3, 5; Book of Mormon: The Testimony of Three Witnesses

Joseph was very happy. The three witnesses would tell other people the gold plates were real. Now people would know Joseph told the truth about the plates.

Jesus told Joseph to show the plates to eight more witnesses. The eight men held the gold plates in their hands. They saw the writing on the plates.

Book of Mormon: The Testimony of Eight Witnesses

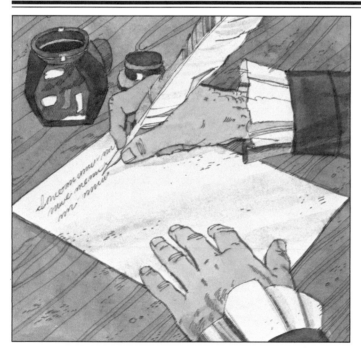

All the witnesses wrote about the gold plates. They said they saw the plates. They said the gold plates were real. The words the witnesses wrote are in the Book of Mormon.

Book of Mormon: The Testimony of Three Witnesses;
The Testimony of Eight Witnesses

Joseph Smith had translated the plates. The witnesses had seen them. Joseph did not need the gold plates any longer. The Angel Moroni came to Joseph. Joseph gave the gold plates back to Moroni.

Now the Book of Mormon was ready to be printed. Joseph took it to a printer. Joseph did not have money to pay the printer. Martin Harris had a lot of money. Jesus said Martin Harris should share his money to pay the printer.

D&C 19:26, 35

Satan did not want the Book of Mormon to be printed. He did not want people to read it. Wicked men tried to stop the printer.

The printer did not work on Sundays. One wicked man went to the printing shop on Sundays. He stole some pages of the Book of Mormon. He printed the pages in a newspaper. Good men made him stop stealing the pages.

Jesus wanted people to read the Book of Mormon. Wicked men cannot stop Jesus' work. The wicked men could not stop the printer. At last the Book of Mormon was printed. Now many people could read it. They could learn the gospel of Jesus Christ.

Getting Ready for the Church of Jesus Christ

Chapter 8 (March–April 1830)

It was almost time for the true Church of Jesus Christ to be on earth again. Jesus gave Joseph Smith a revelation for the people. Jesus wanted the people to be ready for his church. He told them things they must know before they started his church. He told them more about his gospel.

D&C 20:1–4

Jesus said the Book of Mormon teaches his gospel. He said the Book of Mormon is true. Jesus wants people to believe the Book of Mormon. It helps them obey God.

D&C 20:8–15

Jesus told about his life. God sent Jesus to help the people on earth. Satan tried to make him do bad things. But Jesus would not listen to Satan.

D&C 20:21–22

Jesus was sorry for the bad things people do. He bled and suffered for all people. People will not suffer if they repent.

D&C 19:16, 18

Wicked people put Jesus on a cross and killed him.

D&C 20:23

Jesus' friends buried him in a tomb.

Matthew 27:57–61

After three days Jesus was resurrected. He came back to life.

D&C 20:23

Jesus did these things to help people who repent. He died to help
people who have faith and are baptized. They will not be punished. They
can go to heaven. People who do not repent will be punished.

D&C 19:17; 20:25

Jesus told about baptism. People who want to be baptized must repent. They must love and obey Jesus Christ. They must be eight years old or older. Then they can be baptized and be members of the Church.

D&C 20:37, 71; 68:27

Jesus taught the right way to baptize. He said a priest in the Aaronic Priesthood or a man who has the Melchizedek Priesthood may baptize a person. The man who has the priesthood takes the person into the water. He says a special prayer.

D&C 20:72–73

The man who has the priesthood puts the person down under the water. Then he brings the person out of the water.

D&C 20:74

Jesus said people promise to obey him when they are baptized. They must say and do good things.

D&C 20:69

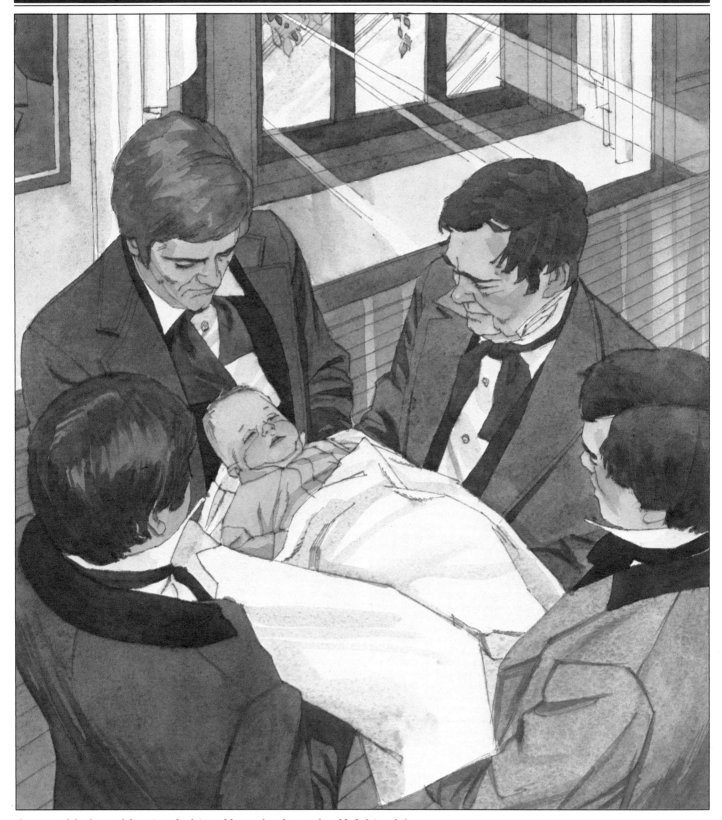

Jesus told about blessing babies. Men who have the Melchizedek
Priesthood can bless babies. The men hold the baby in their arms. One
man gives the baby a name and a blessing.

D&C 20:70

Jesus told about the sacrament. He said the people should take the sacrament often. If we do something bad, we should not take the sacrament. We should repent. Then we may have the sacrament.

D&C 20:75; 46:4

We take the sacrament to remember Jesus. The bread helps us think of Jesus Christ's body. We remember that he died for us on the cross.

D&C 20:77

The water helps us think of the blood of Jesus. We remember that he bled and suffered for us in the Garden of Gethsemane.

D&C 20:79

We make covenants when we take the sacrament. A covenant is a promise. We promise that we will try to be like him. We promise that we will always remember him. We promise to obey his commandments. His Spirit will be with us if we keep our covenants.

D&C 20:77, 79

The True Church of Jesus Christ

Chapter 9 (6 April 1830)

Joseph Smith was living in a town called Fayette. Fayette was in the state of New York. Jesus Christ told Joseph it was time for the true church to be on earth again. Jesus told Joseph to start the Church.

D&C 20:1–2; 21:3

Joseph Smith obeyed. On 6 April 1830, he had a meeting. Five men came to the meeting to help Joseph start the Church. The men were Oliver Cowdery, Hyrum Smith, Samuel Smith, David Whitmer, and Peter Whitmer. They had all been baptized. Other people came to watch the meeting.

The men prayed to Heavenly Father. Joseph ordained Oliver an elder in the Church. Then Oliver ordained Joseph.

Joseph and Oliver blessed the sacrament. They gave it to the men.

Joseph and Oliver put their hands on each man's head. They confirmed the men to be members of the Church of Jesus Christ. They gave the men the gift of the Holy Ghost. They thanked God.

Other people were also at the meeting. Joseph and Oliver ordained some of the men. He gave them the priesthood. The men who were ordained were very happy. They said they loved God. They told how God had blessed them.

Jesus gave a revelation to Joseph Smith at the meeting. Jesus said Joseph was a prophet. When a prophet speaks, he speaks for Jesus. The members of the Church should listen to the prophet. They should obey him.

D&C 21:1, 4–5

After the meeting many people were baptized. Joseph Smith's mother and father were baptized. 6 April 1830 was a wonderful day. The true Church of Jesus Christ was on the earth again.

The First Miracle in the Church

Chapter 10 (April 1830)

The next meeting of the Church of Jesus Christ was on Sunday, 11 April 1830. The members of the Church came to the meeting. The members were called Saints.

Many other people came to the meeting. They were not members of the Church. Oliver Cowdery taught them the gospel of Jesus Christ. Some of the people believed Oliver and wanted to join the Church. They were baptized after the meeting.

Satan did not want people to join the Church. Satan tried to make some of the good people feel bad. One of these people was a man named Newel Knight. Newel Knight was not a member of the Church. Satan did not want him to be baptized.

Joseph asked Newel to say the prayer at a meeting. Newel said he would pray.

Satan did not want Newel to obey Joseph. Newel went to the meeting, but he would not pray. He said he was afraid to pray out loud.

Later Newel Knight went into the woods. He wanted to pray alone. Satan did not want him to pray. Newel tried to pray, but he could not talk. He became sick. He was sad and afraid. Newel went home.

Newel's wife was worried about him. She asked Joseph Smith to help Newel. Joseph Smith used his priesthood power to bless Newel. Then Newel felt good again. He was not sick. He was not afraid. He was happy. Satan could not hurt him. Later Newel Knight was baptized.

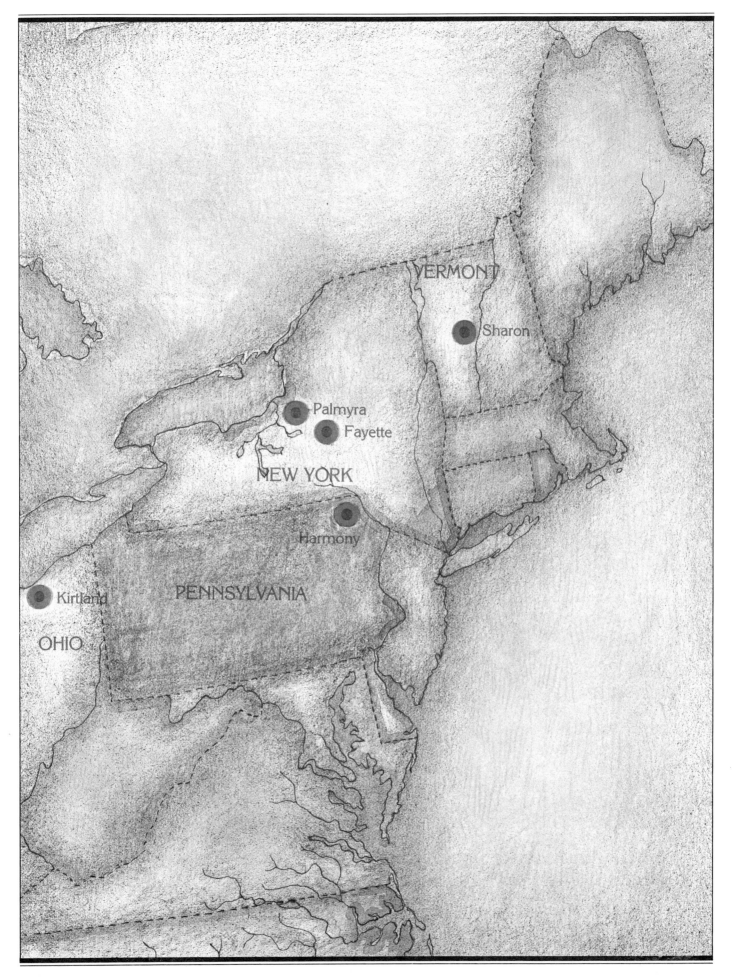

VERMONT

Sharon

Palmyra

Fayette

NEW YORK

Harmony

Kirtland

PENNSYLVANIA

OHIO

More People Join the Church

Chapter 11 (April–June 1830)

Many weeks went by. There were twenty-seven members of the Church. They did not all live in the same town. Joseph Smith asked them to come to a conference. A conference is a special meeting for all the Saints. Saints are members of the Church of Jesus Christ.

The Saints had the sacrament at the conference. Some men were ordained to the priesthood. The Holy Ghost blessed the saints. They were very happy.

Some other people were at the conference. They were not members of the Church. They learned about the gospel at the conference. They wanted to join the Church. They were baptized. After the conference, Joseph Smith went to another town. Some good people there wanted to be baptized. Joseph said they could be baptized in a stream of water.

The people built a small dam in the stream. They made a nice place to be baptized. In the night, some wicked people destroyed the dam.

The good people built the dam again. Then Oliver Cowdery began to baptize them. Soon a mob came. A mob is a crowd of mean, wicked people. The mob said mean things to the good people. The mob tried to hurt them. But the Lord kept the good people safe.

Satan wanted the mob to make trouble for the Church of Jesus Christ. The wicked people told lies about Joseph Smith. They said he did bad things. Joseph was put in jail.

Mean people tried to hurt Joseph. They spit on him. They would not give him food. Some of them told lies about Joseph. But good people told the truth about Joseph. They said he was a righteous man. At last Joseph was let out of jail.

Samuel Smith's Mission

Chapter 12 (June 1830)

Samuel Smith was Joseph Smith's younger brother. Joseph said Jesus wanted Samuel to go on a mission. Samuel Smith was the first missionary for the Church.

Samuel went to teach people the gospel. He wanted to tell them about the Book of Mormon. He tried to sell the book to people. But no one wanted to read it. Samuel was sad.

Samuel's mission was hard. Many times he was hungry. Sometimes he had no place to sleep. Some people were mean to him.

Samuel sold a Book of Mormon to a man named Phineas Young. Phineas read the book. He gave the Book of Mormon to his brother. His brother's name was Brigham Young.

Brigham Young read the Book of Mormon. He believed it was true. He learned about the gospel of Jesus Christ. Phineas and Brigham Young told some friends about the Book of Mormon. Their friends read it. Phineas and Brigham Young and their friends joined the Church.

Later Brigham Young became a prophet of the Church. He helped the Saints. He was a great leader.

Samuel Smith went home. He did not think his mission had helped the Church. He did not know Brigham Young would one day become a prophet.

One night Samuel stopped at an inn. He asked the owner to buy a Book of Mormon. The owner asked where Samuel got the book. Samuel said his brother translated it from some gold plates.

The owner was angry. He said Samuel was lying. He told Samuel to get out of the inn.

That night Samuel had to sleep under an apple tree.

At last Samuel gave a Book of Mormon to a leader of another church. The leader and his wife read the book. They knew it was important.

Joseph and Emma

Chapter 13 (July 1830)

Joseph and Emma Smith lived in Pennsylvania. They had a small farm. Joseph and Emma loved each other. They worked hard to help each other.

Joseph and Emma had many troubles. They were poor. They wanted to have children. Emma had a baby boy, but he died. Emma was sad. Later she and Joseph had more children.

Joseph worried about his family. He wanted to take care of them. He needed to plant crops so his family would have food.

Joseph also worried about the Church. Wicked people were making trouble for the Saints. Some of the Church leaders had to hide from the wicked people. Joseph needed to work hard to help the Saints.

Sometimes Joseph had to leave home to help the Saints. Joseph was sorry to leave his family. Emma was sad when Joseph went away. She worried about him.

Joseph asked Jesus what he should do. Jesus told the prophet Joseph not to worry about his troubles. Jesus told him not to be afraid of wicked people. Jesus said he would always help Joseph.

D&C 24:16–17

Jesus said Joseph should plant crops for his family. Then he should go and help the Saints. Jesus told Joseph not to worry about food, clothes, or money. The Saints would give Joseph what he needed.

D&C 24:3, 18

Jesus gave Joseph Smith a revelation for Emma. Jesus said Emma Smith was a special lady. He had chosen her to do important work.

D&C 25:3

Jesus said Emma should be kind to Joseph when he had troubles. She should help him be happy and not worry.

D&C 25:5

Jesus said Emma Smith should teach the Saints. She should help them learn the scriptures. He said the Holy Ghost would help her know what to teach.

D&C 25:7–8

Jesus said Emma should use her time to study. She should learn and write many things.

D&C 25:8

Jesus asked Emma to choose songs for the Saints to sing. The songs would be printed in a song book.

D&C 25:11

God loves to hear righteous people sing. Their songs are a prayer to him. Righteous people who sing to God will be blessed.

D&C 25:12

Jesus told Emma to be humble. He told her to love her husband. He told her to be happy because Joseph would have many great blessings.

D&C 25:14

Jesus told Emma not to worry about this world. She should get ready for a better world in heaven. She should be happy and obey God's commandments. Then she could go to heaven.

D&C 25:13, 15

Jesus said the things he told Emma Smith are for all women.

D&C 25:16

The Prophet and Revelations for the Church

Chapter 14 (September 1830)

Joseph Smith and Emma moved to New York. A man named Hiram Page lived there. He was a member of the Church. He had a stone. He said the stone helped him have revelations for the Church.

Many Church members believed Hiram Page. Oliver Cowdery believed him. Some people thought Hiram was a prophet.

D&C 28: Preface

Oliver asked Joseph about Hiram Page. Joseph prayed. Jesus gave Joseph a revelation for Oliver Cowdery. He said that only one man could have revelations for the Church. That man was the Prophet Joseph Smith.

D&C 28:2

Jesus said people could have revelations for themselves. But only the prophet could have revelations for the whole Church. Oliver believed Joseph. He knew Hiram Page's revelations were wrong.

D&C 28:1–2, 8

Then Jesus told Oliver to talk to Hiram Page. Oliver told Hiram his revelations were not from God. The revelations were from Satan.

D&C 28:11

Oliver said Satan had tricked Hiram Page. Hiram listened to Oliver. He repented.

Only one man gets revelations for the Church. That man is the President of the Church. He is the leader of the Church. He is the prophet of God. Members of the Church should obey the prophet.

A Mission to the Lamanites

Chapter 15 (September 1830)

Jesus wanted more people to hear about the gospel. He wanted some of the Saints to go on missions. He told Oliver Cowdery to go on a mission to the Indians.

The Indians are called Lamanites in the Book of Mormon. Jesus wanted the Lamanites to read the Book of Mormon. He had promised many prophets that the Lamanites would have the Book of Mormon. Now it was time to keep that promise.

D&C 3:19–20

The Book of Mormon would tell the Lamanites about their ancestors who lived 2,000 years ago. It would tell the Lamanites the promises Jesus made to them. It would help them believe in Jesus and the gospel. It would teach them to repent and be baptized.

D&C 3:19–20

Other men wanted to go with Oliver Cowdery. They wanted to preach the gospel to the Lamanites. They wanted to give the Lamanites the Book of Mormon. The Lord said three of the men could go.

First the missionaries went to some Indians in New York. They found only a few Indians who could read. The missionaries gave them the Book of Mormon.

Then the missionaries went to preach to some Indians in Ohio. The Indians were happy to hear about the Book of Mormon. They were happy to know about their ancestors.

The missionaries left Ohio. They went to a city named Independence, in Jackson County, Missouri. There were many Indians in Missouri.

The missionaries preached the gospel to them. They gave the Indians the Book of Mormon. It made the Indians very happy. They thanked the missionaries for the Book of Mormon.

Other people in Missouri did not believe the gospel. They did not believe the Book of Mormon. They told the missionaries to stay away from the Indians.

The people said soldiers would chase the missionaries away if they did not leave. The missionaries were made sad by this news. They went to teach the gospel to other people in Missouri.

One of the missionaries was named Parley P. Pratt. He went to tell Joseph what they had done. Parley said they had a good mission. They had taught the gospel to many people.

Joseph Smith and Sidney Rigdon Learn about Zion

Chapter 16 (1830)

While Oliver Cowdery and his friends were on their mission, they stopped near Kirtland, Ohio. They met a man named Sidney Rigdon. He was a leader in another church.

The missionaries gave Sidney the Book of Mormon. They taught him the gospel. Sidney Rigdon read the Book of Mormon. He prayed about it. Heavenly Father told him the gospel was true. Sidney Rigdon was baptized.

Sidney Rigdon told the members of his church to listen to the missionaries. Many of them were baptized. Soon 1,000 people were baptized in Kirtland.

Sidney Rigdon wanted to meet Joseph Smith. He went to New York to visit the prophet. Jesus gave Joseph Smith a revelation for Sidney Rigdon. Jesus said Sidney Rigdon would do important things. He would teach the gospel to many people. He would baptize them and give them the gift of the Holy Ghost.

D&C 35:4–6

Jesus told Joseph and Sidney that some parts of the Bible had been changed many years ago. Some important stories were not in the Bible. Jesus would tell Joseph Smith the stories that were not in the Bible. Sidney Rigdon should write them down.

D&C 35:20

One of the stories told about Enoch. Enoch was a great prophet. He taught his people to be very righteous. The Lord called Enoch's righteous people Zion. Enoch's people built a city. They named the city Zion. In Zion, people loved each other. They took care of each other. No one was poor or unhappy.

Moses 7:18–19

Everyone in Zion obeyed Heavenly Father's commandments. The people were so righteous that Jesus came and lived with them. Then God took the people of Zion to heaven to live with him.

Moses 7:69

Jesus told Joseph Smith to teach his people to be righteous. They should try to build another city named Zion. The city would be beautiful. Everyone there would love Heavenly Father. Everyone would love each other. Everyone in Zion would be very happy. Jesus would come and live with them.

D&C 45:64–71

The First Bishops of the Church

Chapter 17 (February 1831)

Some wicked people lived in New York. They were mean to the members of the Church and wanted them to leave. Jesus told Joseph Smith to leave New York and go to Kirtland, Ohio.

Joseph Smith, his wife Emma, Sidney Rigdon, and Edward Partridge went to Kirtland. Joseph and Emma lived with a member of the Church. His name was Newell K. Whitney.

There were 1,000 members of the Church in Kirtland. They were trying to obey God. But they did not understand all of the gospel.

D&C 41: Preface

Joseph prayed to Heavenly Father. Jesus gave Joseph a revelation. Jesus told Joseph the Saints in Kirtland needed a bishop. The bishop should use his time to teach and help the Saints. The first bishop in the Church was Edward Partridge.

D&C 41:9

Jesus told Joseph what a bishop in the Church should do. The bishop should take care of a storehouse. The Saints should put food and clothing in the storehouse. If any Saint needed food or clothing, the bishop should give it to him.

D&C 72:10–12

The bishop should take care of money for the Church. The Saints should give money to the bishop. The bishop should pay the bills for the Church. He should give some of the money to poor Saints.

D&C 72:10–12

The bishop should love the Saints. He should try to help them. He should meet with the men who have the priesthood. They should talk about what they are doing to help the Saints.

D&C 72:5, 11

More people joined the Church. The Church needed more bishops. Newell K. Whitney was the second bishop of the Church.

D&C 72:8

A bishop is the leader of the Saints in each ward. A branch president is like a bishop. A branch president is the leader of the Saints in each branch.

Today there are thousands of bishops in the Church.

The Law of the Church

Chapter 18 (4 February 1831)

In Kirtland the Lord gave a very important revelation to Joseph Smith. It is called the law of the Church.

D&C 42: Preface

The Lord said Saints should teach the gospel to all people. Men who go on missions should be ordained to the priesthood. They should be ordained by leaders of the Church.

D&C 42: Preface, 7, 11

Two missionaries should work together. They should teach from the Bible and the Book of Mormon. They should pray to have the Holy Ghost with them. The Holy Ghost will tell them what to teach.

D&C 42:6, 14

Missionaries should baptize people who believe the gospel.

D&C 42:7

The Lord said members of the Church should obey the Ten Commandments. They should not kill. They should not tell lies. They should not say bad things about other people. They should not do any other bad things.

D&C 42:18–27

The Saints should share what they have with other people. Sharing with others is like sharing with Jesus.

D&C 42:30–38

Jesus gave the Saints other commandments. No Saint should think he is better than another person. The Saints should be clean. They should work hard.

D&C 42:40–42

The Saints should take care of sick members. Men who have the priesthood should bless sick members. Sick members who have faith can be healed. They will not die if it is not time for them to die.

D&C 42:43–44, 48

Righteous Saints should not be afraid to die. Death is wonderful for righteous people.

D&C 42:46

Jesus will give many revelations to righteous members. He will teach them many things. They will know how to be very happy. The Lord told the Saints to obey the law of the Church.

D&C 42:61–62, 66

The Second Coming of Jesus Christ

Chapter 19 (February–March 1831)

Some people in Kirtland, Ohio, were telling lies about the Saints. These people did not want to learn the gospel.

D&C 45: Preface

Jesus told Joseph Smith He would come to earth again soon. Before He comes, everyone on earth must hear the gospel. The Saints should work hard to teach the gospel. They should be good missionaries.

D&C 43: Preface, 20, 45

When Jesus lived on earth, he told his Apostles what would happen before he came again.

D&C 45:16

Jesus told his Apostles that the temple in Jerusalem would be
destroyed. The Jews would have to live in other lands. Many Jews would
be killed. There would be many wars. People would not love each other.
The true church would not be on the earth.

D&C 45:17–24, 27

Then Heavenly Father would start the true church on earth again. The gospel of Jesus Christ would be like a light in the darkness.

D&C 45:28

Many things that Jesus told about have already happened. He told about other things that will still happen. Many people will fight with each other. Many people will be sick. There will be earthquakes. The sun will be dark. The moon will be like blood. Stars will fall.

D&C 45:26, 29, 31, 33, 42

When these things happen, righteous people will know Jesus is coming soon. They will want him to come. Many Jews will go back to Jerusalem. They will hear the gospel.

D&C 45:25, 38–39

Righteous Saints will build the new city of Zion. They will be safe in Zion. They will not fight with each other. They will be very happy. They will sing songs of joy. Wicked people will not be able to go to Zion.

D&C 45:65–71

Jesus will come to earth again. The righteous people will see him. He
will come in a bright cloud. All the righteous people who have died will
be resurrected. They will meet Jesus in the cloud. They will come to
earth with him.

D&C 45:44–46

Jesus will come to Jerusalem. He will stand on a mountain there. The
mountain will split in half. The earth will shake. The heavens will shake.
Wicked people will be destroyed.

D&C 45:48–50

People in Jerusalem will see Jesus. They will ask, "What are those
wounds in your hands and feet?" He will say: "I am Jesus who was
crucified. I am the Son of God." Then the people will cry. They will feel
sad that Jesus was crucified.

D&C 45:51–53

Righteous people will be very happy to see Jesus. The whole earth will belong to them. They will not let Satan tempt them. They will be strong. They will have many children. Their children will grow up and obey God. Jesus will live with the righteous people for 1,000 years. He will be their king.

D&C 45:56–59

Jesus told Joseph Smith to send missionaries to teach everyone about
His coming. He said the Saints should get ready. They should pray and
fast. They should teach each other the commandments.

D&C 43:19–21; 88:77

Jesus said the Saints should try to be close to him.
Then he will be close to them. If Saints ask God for
help, he will help them.

D&C 88:63

The Saints should do everything they can to help
Jesus. When people help Jesus, they become like him.
Then they will be ready for his second coming.

Moroni 7:48

Gifts of the Holy Ghost

Chapter 20 (8 March 1831)

Some of the Saints did not understand about the Holy Ghost. Jesus told Joseph Smith about the Holy Ghost. The Holy Ghost helps Heavenly Father and Jesus. The Holy Ghost does not have a body of flesh and bones. He is a spirit.

D&C 130:22

Jesus said the Holy Ghost helps righteous people. He helps God give them special gifts. Each Saint has a special gift. The Saints should use their gifts to help each other. Jesus told Joseph Smith what the gifts are.

D&C 46:9–12

The Holy Ghost gives some Saints the gift of testimony. They know that Jesus Christ is the Son of God. They know he died for us. Other Saints are given the gift to believe testimonies about Jesus.

D&C 46:13–14

Some Saints are given the gift to be leaders.

D&C 46:15

Some Saints are given the gift to know which spirits are righteous and which spirits are wicked. Righteous spirits are sent by God. They make us feel happy. They are like light. Wicked spirits are sent by Satan. They make us feel mean. They are like darkness.

D&C 46:16, 23; 50:23—24

The Holy Ghost gives some Saints the gift to be wise. They are able to make good choices. Some Saints are given the gift of learning things. They can teach what they know to other Saints. They can teach other Saints to make good choices.

D&C 46:18

Some Saints are given the gift of faith to be healed. Other Saints are given the gift to heal sick people. The Holy Ghost gives some Saints the gift to do miracles. Miracles show the power of God.

D&C 46:19–21

Other Saints are given the gift to speak languages they do not know.

D&C 46:24

The Holy Ghost gives some Saints the gift to know what will happen before it happens.

D&C 46:22

Some Saints are given many gifts.

D&C 46:29

The bishop knows what gifts each Saint has. He knows who will be good teachers. He knows who can do miracles. He knows which Saints love God and obey God's commandments.

D&C 46:27

Righteous Saints can have many gifts. They should work to get the gifts they need. All these gifts come from God.

D&C 46:9, 28, 32

The Prophet Goes to Missouri

Chapter 21 (May–June 1831)

Many of the Saints still lived in New York. Joseph Smith and Sidney Rigdon were in Kirtland, Ohio. Joseph told the Saints in New York to come to Ohio. They obeyed the Prophet. They went to Ohio.

Jesus told Joseph the Saints in Kirtland should share their land with the Saints from New York. Leman Copley had a lot of land. He promised to share it. The Saints from New York moved onto the land.

D&C 48:2

Leman Copely did not keep his promise. He did not want the Saints from New York to have his land. They had to move. They had no place to live.

Newell Knight was their leader. He did not know what to do. He went to see the Prophet Joseph. He asked Joseph what the Saints should do.

The Lord told Joseph the Saints from New York should move to Missouri soon.

D&C 54:7–9

Before they left, the Saints had a conference in Kirtland. The conference lasted three days. The Lord gave some important revelations to Joseph Smith.

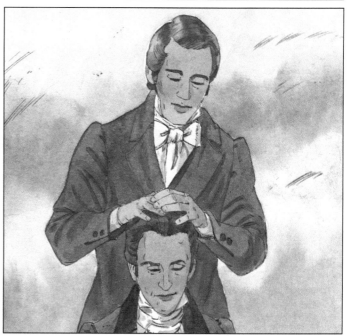

The Lord told Joseph to ordain the first high priests in the Church. High priests have the Melchizedek Priesthood. They are leaders in the Church. Many of the leaders of the Church were ordained high priests.

The Lord said some of the men should go on missions to Missouri. They should preach the gospel on the way. When the conference was over, the missionaries went to Missouri.

D&C 52:9–10

The Lord told Joseph the next conference of the Church would be in Jackson County, Missouri. He told Joseph and his friends to go there. Zion would be built in Jackson County. Jesus would show them where to build the city of Zion.

D&C 52:1–5

The Saints in Missouri

Chapter 22 (July–August 1831)

The Prophet Joseph Smith, Sidney Rigdon, Edward Partridge, and others went to Missouri. They were very happy to go. They wanted to build the city of Zion. They wanted the Lord to show them the right place.

They went part of the way in a boat. When they got to Missouri, Joseph wanted to walk. He knew the land of Missouri was sacred. He wanted to see it.

Joseph and his friends walked 300 miles to Jackson County. It was hot, but they did not care. They wanted to go there to build Zion.

The prophet and his friends went to Jackson County, Missouri. The missionaries from Kirtland met them.

A few days later, the Saints from New York also went to Jackson County. Everyone was happy to be there.

The Prophet Joseph and Bishop Edward Partridge told the people what to do. Some should buy land in Missouri. Oliver Cowdery and William W. Phelps should start schools. They should write books little children could read.

D&C 55:4

Joseph wanted to know where the city of Zion should be built. He prayed to Heavenly Father. His prayer was answered.

The Lord said Zion would be built near the city of Independence in
Jackson County, Missouri. The Lord told Joseph where to build a
temple. He said Zion would not be built soon. The Saints would have
many troubles first. But they could build Zion if they had enough faith.

D&C 57:1–3; 58:2–4

The Lord told Joseph the Saints should obey the law in Missouri. They should obey God's commandments. They should do many good things without being told. The Saints should repent of their sins. The Lord does not remember sins when people repent.

D&C 58:21, 27–29, 42

The Lord said that Sidney Rigdon should dedicate the land. Sidney Rigdon asked the Saints if they were thankful for the land. He asked if they would obey all God's commandments. The Saints said, "Yes." Then Sidney Rigdon prayed and dedicated the land.

D&C 58:57

The next day Joseph Smith, Oliver Cowdery, Sidney Rigdon, and some of their friends had a meeting. They met at a special place in Independence. They read the scriptures. Then they prayed. Joseph Smith dedicated the place for a temple to be built.

All the Saints in Missouri went to a conference. They were filled with the Holy Ghost. Joseph told the Saints God would bless them if they kept their promises.

A few days later Jesus gave Joseph another revelation. He said Sunday is a special day. Sunday is the day we should do things to help us remember Jesus. We should not work on Sunday. We should go to Church and take the sacrament. We should repent of our sins. We should visit the sick. We should be thankful for all our blessings. We should always obey God's commandments.

D&C 59:3–15

Saints who do these things will have all the good things they need. They will have food, clothes, houses, and gardens. They will be happy. They will have peace in this life. They will have eternal life.

D&C 59:15–19, 23

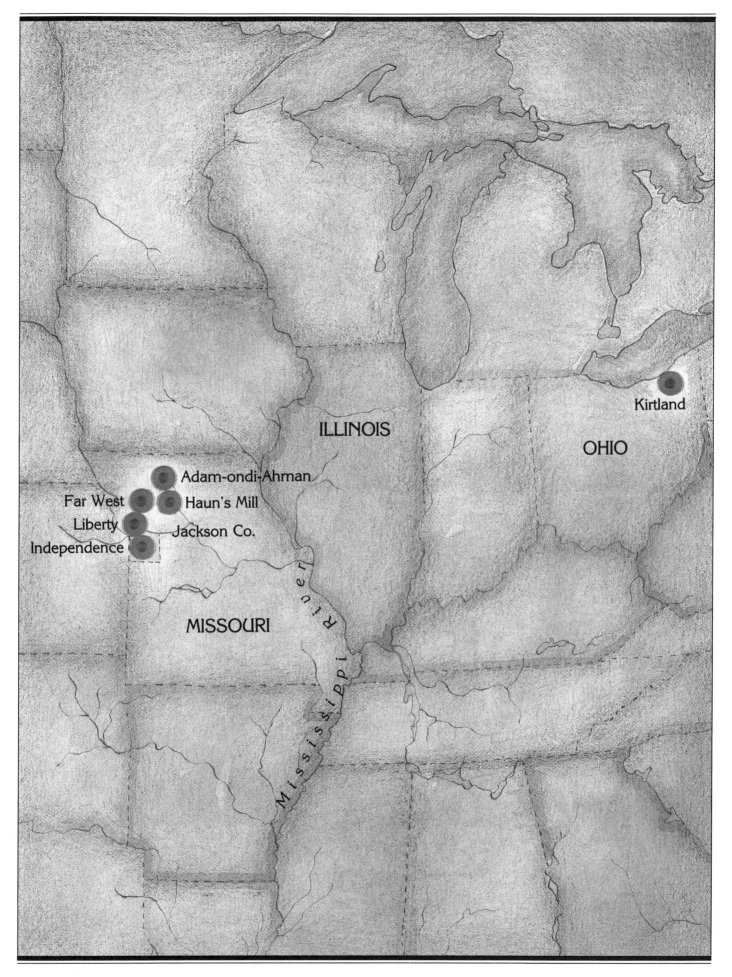

Kirtland

ILLINOIS

OHIO

Adam-ondi-Ahman

Far West   Haun's Mill

Liberty   Jackson Co.

Independence

MISSOURI

Mississippi River

The Doctrine and Covenants

Chapter 23 (August–November 1831)

Joseph Smith and some of the Saints left Missouri. They went back to Kirtland, Ohio. The Saints had a conference in Ohio.

The Lord had given Joseph Smith many revelations. Joseph had written the revelations. The Saints wanted to put the revelations in a book. The book would be named the Book of Commandments. Later it was called the Doctrine and Covenants.

Jesus told Joseph the revelations were very important. They came from God. Everything in them is true. Jesus gave Joseph two more revelations. One revelation was for the beginning of the Doctrine and Covenants. One was for the end. They tell us that the Doctrine and Covenants is an important book.

D&C 67: Preface; 133: Preface

The Doctrine and Covenants tells everyone that the true Church of Jesus Christ is on the earth again.

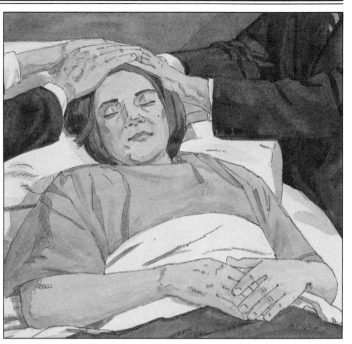

The Doctrine and Covenants tells about the priesthood. Righteous men have priesthood power again.

The Doctrine and Covenants tells about the Book of Mormon. People can read the Book of Mormon. Everyone can know about the gospel of Jesus Christ.

The Doctrine and Covenants also teaches the Saints to share. Saints who share will be filled with the Holy Ghost.

D&C 70:14

The Doctrine and Covenants teaches the commandments of God. Saints who obey these commandments can build Zion. They can live with Heavenly Father and Jesus forever.

Jesus said all the members of the Church should read the Doctrine and Covenants.

D&C 1:37

After the conference Oliver Cowdery went to Missouri. He took the revelations that Joseph had written. He gave them to a printer. He told the printer to print 3,000 books, but wicked men stopped the press and destroyed most of the pages.

The Saints thanked Heavenly Father for the revelations in the Doctrine and Covenants. They promised they would tell other people the revelations came from God.

Parents Should Teach Their Children

Chapter 24 (November 1831)

Some Saints in Ohio went to see Joseph Smith. Jesus gave Joseph a revelation for them. Jesus told the Saints how to be good parents.

D&C 68: Preface

Jesus said children should be baptized when they are eight years old. Jesus commanded parents to teach their children the gospel before they are baptized.

D&C 68:25

Children should know about Jesus. They should have faith in him.

D&C 68:25

Children should know how to repent.

D&C 68:25

Children should know about baptism. They should learn to be good members of the Church.

D&C 68:25, 28

Children should know how to pray. They should know how to listen to the Holy Ghost.

D&C 68:28

Children should know God's commandments. They should obey the commandments.

D&C 68:28

Parents must teach their children these things. Parents will be blamed for their children's sins if they do not teach them the gospel.

D&C 68:25

Joseph Smith and Sidney Rigdon Go on a Mission

Chapter 25 (December 1831–January 1832)

Some people did not like the Church of Jesus Christ. They told lies about it. Some of the lies were printed in a newspaper. Jesus told Joseph Smith and Sidney Rigdon to go on a mission to other towns. They could tell people the truth about the Church.

D&C 71:1–4

Joseph and Sidney obeyed Jesus. They left their homes. They went to many towns. Joseph and Sidney talked in church meetings. They taught people in their homes.

Joseph and Sidney told people about God's commandments. They told people about their testimonies of Jesus Christ. They told the people to repent. Joseph and Sidney finished their missionary work. They went home to their families.

The Three Kingdoms of Heaven

Chapter 26 (16 February 1832)

One day Joseph Smith and Sidney Rigdon were reading the New Testament. The New Testament said good people go to heaven after they are resurrected. Joseph wondered if all people go to the same place in heaven. Joseph and Sidney prayed. They asked Heavenly Father to tell them about heaven.

D&C 76: Preface

Heavenly Father answered their prayer. They had a revelation. It was a beautiful vision. In the vision Joseph and Sidney saw heaven. They saw Jesus with light all around him. Then they saw angels around Jesus and Heavenly Father.

D&C 76: Preface, 19–21

Joseph and Sidney said they knew Jesus lived. They saw him! Joseph and Sidney heard a voice. The voice said Jesus was the Son of God. He came to earth. Jesus showed all people how to live so they could be with Heavenly Father again.

D&C 76:22–24

Then Joseph and Sidney saw where people go after they are
resurrected. There are three places for people to go in heaven.
Righteous Saints go to the celestial kingdom of heaven after they are
resurrected. The celestial kingdom is where Heavenly Father and Jesus
live.

D&C 76:50–70

Righteous Saints had faith in Jesus when they lived on earth. They were baptized. The Holy Ghost taught them how to live.

D&C 76:51–54

Righteous Saints had many troubles, but they had faith. Jesus helped them when they had troubles. They worked hard. They repented and obeyed all God's commandments. Satan tempted them, but they did not follow Satan.

D&C 76:51–54

Righteous Saints will become like Heavenly Father and Jesus. They will know everything. They will be perfect. They will become gods.

D&C 76:58–60

Then Joseph and Sidney saw another place. It is named the terrestrial kingdom of heaven. Some people will go to the terrestrial kingdom after they are resurrected.

D&C 76:71

People in the terrestrial kingdom were good people on earth. But they were not righteous Saints. They did not have faith in Jesus. They obeyed some of God's commandments. But they did not obey all of the commandments.

D&C 76:75

They did not believe the gospel when they heard it on earth. After they died they believed the gospel.

D&C 76:73–74

People in the terrestrial kingdom will see Jesus. But they cannot live with Heavenly Father or Jesus. They will not become gods.

D&C 76:77–79

Joseph and Sidney saw a third place. It is named the telestial kingdom of heaven. People who go to the telestial kingdom were not righteous on earth.

D&C 76:81, 103

These people did not believe in Jesus. They did not believe the prophets. They were not baptized. They did not obey God's commandments.

D&C 76:81–82, 102–103

People who go to the telestial kingdom cannot see Jesus or Heavenly Father. Angels will visit them. The Holy Ghost will teach them. People in the telestial kingdom will know about Jesus and Heavenly Father. But they can never live with them.

D&C 76:86

People who are going to the celestial and terrestrial kingdoms will be resurrected when Jesus comes again. People who go to the telestial kingdom will not be resurrected when Jesus comes again. They must wait 1,000 years to be resurrected.

D&C 76:63, 85, 102

Joseph and Sidney saw where wicked people will go. They will be with Satan. They cannot be with Heavenly Father, Jesus, or the Holy Ghost.

D&C 76:35–37

The people who will be with Satan learned the gospel on earth. The Holy Ghost taught them about Jesus Christ.

D&C 76:35

They knew that Jesus lived. They knew Jesus died for us. But then Satan tempted these people. He tried to get them to do wicked things. They obeyed Satan. They stopped listening to the Holy Ghost. They stopped believing in Jesus. They became very wicked. They will live with Satan forever.

D&C 76:31–35

Joseph and Sidney saw other things in their vision. Jesus told them not to write down everything they saw. Very righteous Saints can see these things for themselves. The Holy Ghost will teach them. Joseph and Sidney thanked God for this beautiful vision.

D&C 76:113–119

The Work of the Prophet Joseph Smith

Chapter 27 (March 1832)

Joseph Smith and his wife Emma had twin babies. The babies got sick and died. Joseph's friends also had twin babies, but these twins' mother died. Joseph and Emma adopted the babies and took care of them.

Jesus told Joseph to read the Bible. Men had changed some words in the Bible. Jesus told Joseph the right words to be in the Bible. Sidney Rigdon helped Joseph write the words Jesus wanted in the Bible.

Joseph Smith did not understand some parts of the Bible. He asked God questions. The Lord Jesus Christ answered the questions. Joseph wrote the answers for the Saints to read.

D&C 77, 113

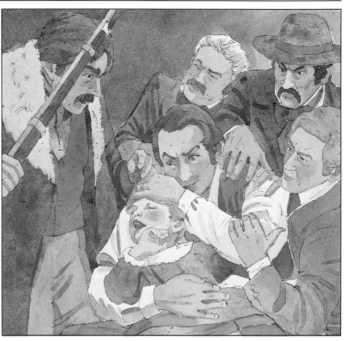

Jesus was happy with Joseph's work. Joseph was a great prophet. But Satan was not happy. Satan wanted to stop Joseph's work. Satan wanted people to be angry at Joseph.

One night, a mob of angry people went to Joseph's home. They broke open the door. They went inside. Joseph was holding one of the little babies. The baby was very sick.

The wicked men grabbed Joseph. The baby was left alone. Later the baby died. The men dragged Joseph outside in the cold winter night. The men choked Joseph.

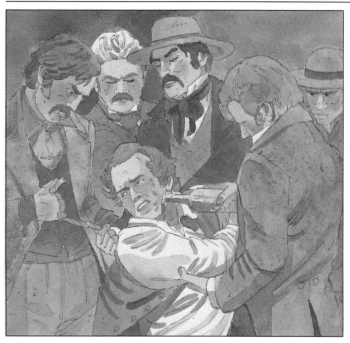

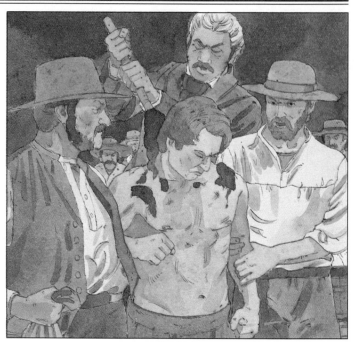

Some men wanted to hurt Joseph. Other men wanted to kill him. They tried to pour poison down his throat. They broke one of his teeth. The poison burned him.

The men tore Joseph's clothes off and smeared tar on him. They covered him with feathers. The feathers stuck to the tar.

Then the mob went away. They thought Joseph would die. Joseph tried to stand up. He could not. He rested for awhile. Then he crawled back to the house.

Joseph's friends cleaned the tar from his body. It was hard to get the tar off. His skin was burned and sore. It hurt.

Joseph Smith did not let the mob stop his work. The next day was Sunday. Joseph went to church. Some of the men in the mob came to the church meeting. They were surprised to see Joseph. Joseph gave a talk in church. Satan had not stopped the Prophet's work.

The Prophet Joseph Goes to Missouri Again

Chapter 28 (March–May 1832)

Jesus gave Joseph Smith a revelation. He said the Saints were like his little children. They were still learning. Jesus said they should be happy. They should be thankful. He would be their leader.

D&C 78:17–18

Jesus wanted the Saints to share with each other. He wanted them to take care of the poor people. Jesus wanted the Saints to help each other.

D&C 78:3–6, 14

Soon after the revelation Joseph went to Missouri again. Missouri was called the land of Zion. Some of Joseph's friends went with him. The Saints in Zion were happy to see Joseph.

Joseph asked the Saints to come to a meeting. He told them about the revelation. The Saints knew Joseph was the Prophet of God.

At the meeting the Lord gave Joseph another revelation for the Saints. Jesus was happy that the Saints had forgiven each other. Jesus said, "I, the Lord, forgive you."

D&C 82:1

Jesus gave the Saints a new commandment. He said he had given them the land of Zion. Now they must share the land with each other. Everyone should have what he needed. This would help the Church of Jesus Christ.

D&C 82:17–20

After the meeting, Joseph visited the Saints in many towns. The Saints were happy to see him. It was a happy time for Joseph. He loved the Saints.

Jesus gave Joseph a revelation about women and children. Jesus said husbands should take care of their wives. Parents should take care of their children.

D&C 83:2, 4

The Saints should take care of women who do not have husbands. The Saints should take care of children who do not have fathers or mothers.

D&C 83:6

Jesus said the Saints should put food in a storehouse. The bishop should give hungry people food from the storehouse.

D&C 83:6

Joseph Smith and Bishop Whitney started back to Kirtland. They rode in a wagon.

One day, something scared the horses. They ran fast.

Joseph jumped from the wagon. He was not hurt. Bishop Whitney jumped from the wagon. He broke his leg.

Joseph Smith and Bishop Whitney stayed at an inn. Bishop Whitney rested for four weeks. Joseph stayed with him while his leg got better.

Someone at the inn put poison in Joseph's food. He was very sick.

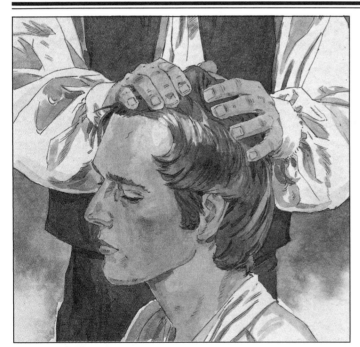

Joseph asked Bishop Whitney to give him a blessing. Bishop Whitney used the power of the priesthood to bless Joseph. Joseph was healed.

Joseph thanked God for healing him. At last, Joseph Smith and Bishop Whitney could travel. They went home to their families.

A Revelation about the Priesthood

Chapter 29 (September 1832)

Many men of the Church went on missions. When they came home they went to see Joseph Smith in Kirtland.

D&C 84: Preface

The men told Joseph about their missions. They had baptized many people. They were happy about their missions. The Prophet Joseph was happy too.

D&C 84: Preface

All of these missionaries had the priesthood. The priesthood is the power of God. The missionaries wanted to know more about the priesthood.

Jesus gave Joseph a revelation for them. Jesus told Joseph about some men who had the Melchizedek Priesthood. Adam had the priesthood. He was the first person to live on the earth.

D&C 84: Preface, 16

All of the Old Testament prophets had the priesthood. Some of the prophets were Enoch, Noah, Moses, Melchizedek, and Abraham. Melchizedek gave the priesthood to Abraham.

D&C 84:6–15

Jesus said men with the priesthood would lead his church. They could baptize and give the gift of the Holy Ghost. They could bless the sacrament. They could give blessings to sick people. All of these things help the Saints get ready to see God.

D&C 84:19–22

Jesus told Joseph that men should be righteous. Then they can have the priesthood. God makes a covenant with them. A covenant is a promise. God promises to bless the men who have the priesthood. The men promise to use the priesthood power to help other people. Men who have the priesthood can become God's special sons. One day Heavenly Father will share all he has with them.

D&C 84:33–39

Jesus told Joseph how men in the Church should use their priesthood. The priesthood can be used only by righteous men. Men should never use the priesthood to be bossy or mean. God will not give priesthood power to mean men.

D&C 121:36–37

Men should use the priesthood with love and kindness. They should listen to the Holy Ghost. Then they will always have priesthood power. The Holy Ghost will be with them forever.

D&C 121:41–43, 45–46

Jesus told Joseph Smith more men should go on missions. They should preach the gospel to all the world. They should teach that God will judge all people. They should teach people to repent. They should baptize people and give them the Holy Ghost.

D&C 84:62–64

Jesus said missionaries will be blessed if they work hard. Angels will help them. Heavenly Father will give them the things they need.

D&C 84:80–88

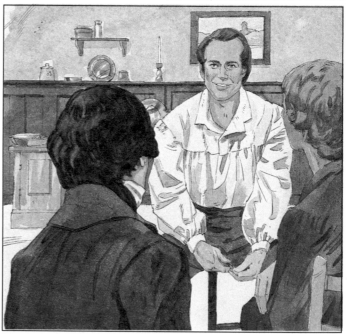

The revelation ended. Joseph and the missionaries were happy to know more about the priesthood. They wanted to use their priesthood power the right way. They wanted to teach others about the Church.

A Revelation about War

Chapter 30 (25 December 1832)

Many people were being baptized into the Church of Jesus Christ. The gospel made them happy. But the Saints worried about things that were happening in other lands.

Sad things were happening in many places in the world. There were earthquakes. People were sick. Many people were dying.

Sad things were also happening in the United States. Some people did not want to be part of the United States. They wanted to have their own leaders.

On Christmas day, 1832, Jesus gave Joseph Smith a revelation. The revelation was about war.

D&C 87

Jesus said there would be a war in the United States. The people in the United States would fight each other.

D&C 87:1–3

Later there would be wars in other lands. There would be fighting in all the world. Jesus said the Saints should be righteous. They should be ready for him to come to earth again.

D&C 87:3–8

Joseph was sad to know there would be wars. He knew people should obey God's commandments. Then they would not fight and have war.

The Word of Wisdom

Chapter 31 (February 1833)

Joseph Smith started a school for men in the Church. It was called the School of the Prophets.

The school was in a room in Newel Whitney's store in Kirtland, Ohio. Joseph taught the men about the Church. He taught them about the priesthood and about the scriptures.

Many of the men smoked pipes or cigars. The room was filled with smoke. Some men chewed tobacco. The floor became dirty. The room needed cleaning when the men went home.

Joseph's wife, Emma, had to clean the room after each meeting. Joseph wondered if men should smoke or chew tobacco.

Joseph prayed and asked God what was right. Jesus gave Joseph a revelation. It was called the Word of Wisdom. Jesus said some people do wicked things. They want other people to do things that are not good for their bodies. In the Word of Wisdom, Jesus told the Saints about things that are good for their bodies. He told about things that are bad for their bodies. The Saints would be blessed if they obeyed the Word of Wisdom.

D&C 89:1, 4

Jesus said alcohol is not good for people. They should not have drinks with alcohol in them. Alcohol should only be used on the outside of the body.

D&C 89:5–7

Jesus said people should not use tobacco. They should not smoke cigarettes, cigars, or pipes. They should not chew tobacco. Jesus said, "Tobacco is not for the body and is not good for man."

D&C 89:8

Jesus said the Saints should not drink hot drinks. Tea and coffee are hot drinks. They are not good for the body.

D&C 89:9

Jesus said many plants and animals are good for people to eat. People should thank Heavenly Father for the good food.

D&C 89:11–12

Jesus said people should not eat too much meat. People should eat meat when the weather is cold. They should eat meat when there is not enough other food.

D&C 89:12, 13

The Lord said all grain is good for our bodies. Some grains are wheat, rice, corn, and oats. Wheat is very good for us. All fruits and vegetables are good for people.

D&C 89:14–17

Jesus said Saints must obey the Word of Wisdom. Then God would bless them. They would have good health. They would be wise. They would be able to learn many things. They would be blessed if they ate the right foods.

D&C 89:18–21

The Church of Jesus Christ in Kirtland

Chapter 32 (March–June 1833)

Joseph Smith was the prophet of the Church of Jesus Christ. The Lord said Joseph should have men to help him. They would be his counselors. His counselors should be Sidney Rigdon and Frederick G. Williams. Joseph and his counselors were the First Presidency of the Church.

D&C 81:1; 90:6

Today the living prophet is the leader of the Church. He and his counselors are called the First Presidency.

Joseph Smith and his counselors were ordained at a meeting in Kirtland, Ohio. It was a sacred meeting. All the people at the meeting had the sacrament.

A few weeks later, Joseph Smith started the first stake of the Church. A stake is many members of the Church who live near each other. All the Saints in Kirtland were in the first stake. Today the Church has many stakes.

Then Jesus said the Saints should build more Church buildings. They should build a temple in Kirtland. They needed to build a place for the First Presidency to work. The Church also needed a printing shop.

D&C 94, 95

The Saints obeyed the Lord. They started to build the Kirtland Temple. It was hard work to build a temple. All the Saints needed to help.

More people joined the Church. Jesus told Joseph to choose more leaders for the Saints. He said Joseph's father should be the Patriarch for the Church. The Patriarch gives blessings to the Saints. He has the Melchizedek Priesthood.

Jesus told Joseph to choose 12 men to be high councilors. They are men who have the Melchizedek Priesthood. They help the Saints know what is right and what is wrong.

D&C 102

A Revelation about Jesus Christ

Chapter 33 (May 1833)

One day Jesus talked to the Prophet Joseph Smith. He told Joseph Smith about himself. Jesus said people can see his face and know him. First they must stop doing wicked things. They must pray and obey God's commandments. Then some day they can see Jesus.

D&C 93:1

Jesus said he is the light of the world. A light shows us the right way to go. Jesus is the light of the world because he shows us the right way to live.

D&C 93:2

Jesus lived with Heavenly Father before the earth was made. Jesus made the earth. He made all things on the earth.

D&C 93:7–10

Jesus was not like his Father in Heaven at first. He did not know all the things his Father knew. He did not have all the power and glory his Father had. He tried hard to be like his Father. Then he became like God, the Father. Jesus had power and glory.

D&C 93:12–17

Jesus said we should obey God's commandments. Then we will learn the truth. We will know all things. Then we can become like God, the Father. We can have power and glory.

D&C 93:20, 27–28

Jesus said Satan does not want people to become like God. He does not want them to know the truth. Jesus told Joseph to teach his family the truth.

D&C 93:39, 47–48

Jesus said Sidney Rigdon and Frederick G. Williams should teach their families to obey God's commandments. Then Satan could not keep their families from knowing the truth.

D&C 93:40–44

God Warns the People of Zion

Chapter 34 (July–August 1833)

God commanded more Saints to go to Jackson County, Missouri. Many people went there to live. They built homes, stores, and a printing shop.

Satan did not want the Saints to live in Jackson County. He did not want them to build the city of Zion. He wanted other people to be mean to them. Satan wanted wicked people to make the Saints leave Jackson County. The wicked people did what Satan wanted. They tried to make the Saints leave.

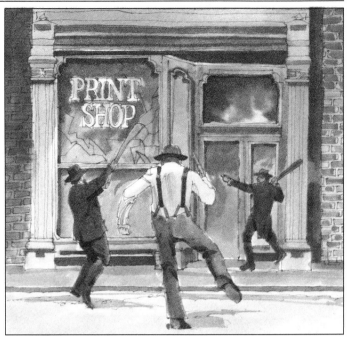

A mob of angry people met. The mob sent some men to see the leaders of the Church. The men told the Saints they must leave Jackson County. But the leaders of the Church knew God wanted them to build the city of Zion in Jackson County. They told the mob the Saints could not leave.

The wicked men went back to the mob. The mob was very angry. They broke into the Saints' printing shop. They destroyed it. The Saints could not print books or newspapers.

The mob caught Bishop Partridge and Brother Allen and took off their clothes. They put hot tar and feathers on their skin. The mob found other Saints and beat them.

Three days later the wicked men rode through the town. They shot their guns at buildings. They shouted mean things at the Saints. They said they would whip anyone they caught. They tried to find the leaders of the Church. The leaders of the Church hid from the mob.

One of the leaders was Oliver Cowdery. He left Jackson County. He went to see Joseph in Kirtland.

Oliver told Joseph what the wicked people were doing in Zion. The Saints in Jackson County wanted to know what they should do.

Joseph told Oliver about some revelations Jesus gave him. The Lord said the Saints should build a temple in Zion. The Saints should pay tithing. The tithing money would pay for the temple. Jesus told Joseph that Zion would become big if the Saints obeyed God. The Saints would be punished if they did not obey God.

D&C 97:10–12, 18, 22–26

Jesus said the Saints should obey the laws of the country. The Saints should vote for righteous people to be the leaders of the land. Sometimes wicked people become the leaders of the land. This makes righteous people unhappy.

D&C 98:4–10

The Lord commanded the Saints to stop doing bad things. Jesus said the Saints should not worry about the mobs. They should not hate the wicked people. The Saints should forgive their enemies. They should fight only when God commanded them to fight. God will punish the wicked people.

D&C 98:11, 14, 23–29, 33, 39–48

Later, Jesus said the Saints in Zion would have trouble for a while. They had not obeyed the commandments. Some day, Jesus would help the Saints build Zion. Then Jesus would bless them.

D&C 100:13–17

The Saints Leave Jackson County, Missouri

Chapter 35 (September–December 1833)

Wicked people were making trouble for the Saints in Jackson County, Missouri. The Saints tried to get help from the governor of Missouri. William Phelps and Orson Hyde went to see the governor. They told him about the mob. They told how their homes had been destroyed.

The governor would not help them. He told them to ask the judges for help. But the judges were friends of the wicked mob. They would not help the Saints.

The mob attacked the Saints for six days. They tore down their homes. They hurt the men. They broke into the store and threw everything on the floor.

The mob made the Saints leave their homes. It was winter time. Many people died because of the cold, wet weather. The Saints went to other towns in Missouri to get away from the mob.

The Saints were sad. Their homes, farms, and stores were destroyed. Their animals were stolen. The governor and the judges would not help the Saints.

But the Saints still had faith in God. They knew the Church of Jesus Christ was the true church. They knew Joseph Smith was a prophet of God.

Joseph Smith was in Kirtland, Ohio. Jesus gave him a revelation. He told Joseph why the Saints had trouble. Some of them had not obeyed God's commandments.

D&C 101:2, 6–7

Jesus said the Saints did not work together. They did not share. They said mean things to each other. They did not pray to God when they were happy. They never thanked God. They only prayed when they needed help.

D&C 101:6–8

Jesus said the Saints should get ready for him to come to earth again. When he comes, people will have peace. The Saints who suffered for Jesus will be blessed. Satan will not have power to tempt the Saints. No one will be sad. No one will die. When Jesus comes again, everyone will be happy.

D&C 101:22, 26–36

Zion's Camp

Chapter 36 (February–June 1834)

While Joseph Smith was in Kirtland, Ohio, he heard the Saints were having trouble in Missouri. The mob had made them leave their homes. The Saints had prayed to Heavenly Father for help.

Jesus gave Joseph Smith a revelation. He said some of the men of the Church should go to Missouri to help the Saints. Joseph Smith would be their leader. They should take money to buy land. The Lord wanted 500 men to go.

D&C 103:21–23, 31–32

Joseph obeyed the Lord. He told the Saints that 500 men should go to the land of Zion in Missouri. He asked the men to come to Kirtland. Only 100 men came. The other men of the Church did not obey the Lord.

The 100 men were called Zion's Camp. They started to the land of Zion. Some of the men walked. Other men rode in wagons. They camped together at night. On the way 100 more men joined them.

The men traveled 1,000 miles. The trip was long and hard. The men did not have enough good food.

Some of the men said the trip was too hard. They did not like the food. They said Joseph Smith was not a good leader. Joseph told these men to repent. If they did not repent, they would get sick and die.

Some of the men were righteous. They helped Joseph Smith. They obeyed God's commandments. They showed how much they loved the Church of Jesus Christ. Joseph Smith would always remember how they helped him.

At last, the men of Zion's Camp got to Missouri. They camped by a river.

The mob knew the men were there. At night the mob came close to the camp. They wanted to kill the men of Zion's Camp.

God sent a terrible storm. The wind blew trees down. Big hailstones fell from the sky. Lightning hit trees. The river water flooded the land. One of the men in the mob was killed by lightning. Other men in the mob were hurt.

The men in the mob were afraid. They knew God was helping the men of Zion's Camp. The mob ran away. They did not hurt the men of Zion's Camp. The storm did not hurt the men of Zion's Camp.

Two days later the Lord gave Joseph Smith a revelation. The Lord said the men in Zion's Camp could stay in Missouri or go back to Kirtland.

D&C 105:20–21

Jesus said some of the men had not obeyed him. He was not happy with them. But some of the men had obeyed. The Lord was happy with them. He said he would bless them with more power.

D&C 105:2–4, 18–19

A few days later many men in Zion's Camp got sick. Fourteen of them died. Joseph had told them they would die if they did not repent.

Joseph Smith met with the Saints in Missouri. He chose men for a high council. Then Joseph and his friends went back to Kirtland.

The men of Zion's Camp did not help the Saints in Missouri. The men could not help because they had not obeyed God. God said Zion can only be built by righteous people.

D&C 105:2–10

Priesthood Leaders

Chapter 37 (February 1835)

Joseph Smith had an important meeting in Kirtland, Ohio. He asked the men of Zion's Camp to come. Joseph told the men Jesus wanted 12 Apostles to help lead his Church.

The Lord had told Oliver Cowdery, David Whitmer, and Martin Harris to choose the Apostles. At the meeting Oliver, David, and Martin were blessed by the First Presidency of the Church. Then they prayed together. They chose 12 good men.

D&C 18:37

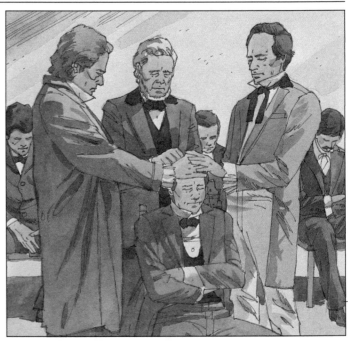

The men were ordained. They were the Twelve Apostles.

Apostles are very important men in the Church. They know that Jesus is our Savior. They teach the gospel all over the world.

D&C 107:23–24

After a few days, other men were chosen to be leaders in the Church. They were called the First Quorum of Seventy. The First Quorum of Seventy help the Apostles. They are the leaders of the missionary work in the Church.

D&C 107:25, 34

One day the Twelve Apostles were in a meeting. They were getting ready to go on missions. They were trying to be righteous. They wanted Heavenly Father's help.

The Apostles asked Joseph Smith to pray for a revelation to help them on their missions. Jesus gave Joseph and the Apostles a great revelation. He told them about the priesthood.

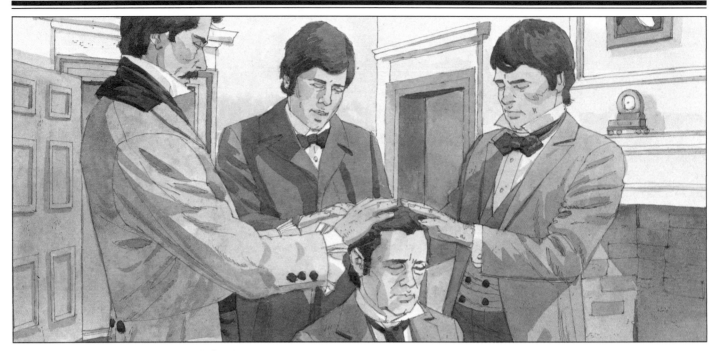

The priesthood is the power of God. It is the greatest power on earth. God gives the priesthood to righteous men. The men use the priesthood to do God's work.

There are two priesthoods in the Church. One is the Melchizedek Priesthood. The Church leaders have the Melchizedek Priesthood. The leaders are the President of the Church and his counselors, the Twelve Apostles, and the First Quorum of Seventy.

D&C 107:1, 22–26

The President of the Church is the prophet of God. He tells people what Jesus wants them to do. The prophet has men who help him. They are his counselors. The prophet and his counselors are the First Presidency of the Church.

D&C 107:22

Other men in the Church have the Melchizedek Priesthood. They are called high priests, seventies, and elders. High priests can be patriarchs, stake presidents, high councilors, and bishops.

D&C 107:5, 7, 9, 10, 17, 25, 39

Some men are chosen to be seventies. They teach the gospel in the wards and stakes.

D&C 107:96–97

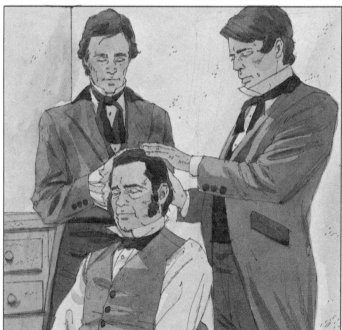

Other men are chosen to be elders. Elders go on missions.

D&C 107:7; 133:8

All men who have the Melchizedek Priesthood can bless people. They can give people the Holy Ghost.

D&C 20:43; 107:18

The other priesthood is the Aaronic Priesthood. Priests, teachers, and deacons have the Aaronic Priesthood. Priests can baptize people. They bless the sacrament. They help the elders.

D&C 20:46–52

Teachers help get the sacrament ready. They go home teaching. They help members of the Church live good lives.

D&C 20:53–57

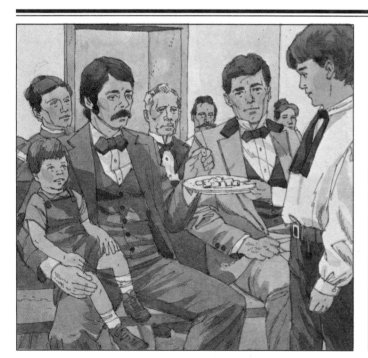

Deacons pass the sacrament. They help the bishop. They collect fast offerings.

Jesus said all men who have the priesthood should learn what God wants them to do. They must work hard. Then Heavenly Father will bless them.

D&C 107:99

The Pearl of Great Price

Chapter 38

The Pearl of Great Price is a book. God helped the prophets write the Pearl of Great Price. It is one of our scriptures. There are four parts to the Pearl of Great Price. They are the Book of Moses, the Book of Abraham, the writings of Joseph Smith, and the Articles of Faith.

The Book of Moses
The first part of the Pearl of Great Price is a revelation given to Joseph Smith. It is named the Book of Moses. Moses was a prophet of God. He lived long ago.

The Book of Moses tells what God said to Moses on a high mountain. Moses saw God and talked to him. God said he had a special work for Moses to do.

God showed Moses the world. Moses saw everything that would happen in the world. He saw all of God's children who would live in the world.

Moses 1:8

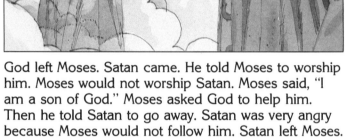

God left Moses. Satan came. He told Moses to worship him. Moses would not worship Satan. Moses said, "I am a son of God." Moses asked God to help him. Then he told Satan to go away. Satan was very angry because Moses would not follow him. Satan left Moses.

Moses 1:9, 12–22

Moses was filled with the Holy Ghost. God came and talked with Moses again. God said the Savior, Jesus Christ, is God's son. God said there are many worlds. Jesus made them. He will make more worlds. There will always be many worlds. God's children will live on them.

Moses 1:24–25, 29–33, 38

Moses learned about God's work. God works to help people so they can live with him forever. He works to help people be like him. The Book of Moses also tells about the prophet Enoch and the city of Zion.

Moses 1:39; 2–8

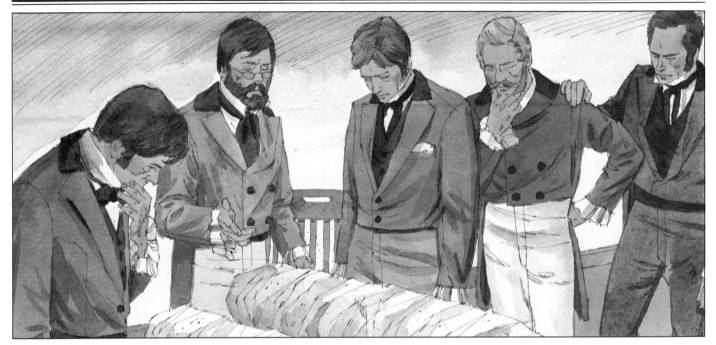

The Book of Abraham

The second part of The Pearl of Great Price is the Book of Abraham.
One day in July 1835, a man named Mr. Chandler came to Kirtland. Mr.
Chandler was showing the people some mummies from Egypt. When
people died in Egypt their bodies were wrapped in cloth. The bodies
were called mummies.

Some rolls of very old paper were with the mummies.
Some strange writing was on the paper. Mr. Chandler
was looking for someone who could read the writing.
He heard that Joseph Smith could translate the writing.

Joseph looked at the writing on the paper. He could
read the writing. He told Mr. Chandler what it said.
Some of the Saints bought the rolls of paper from Mr.
Chandler.

Joseph translated the writing on the paper. Oliver Cowdery and William Phelps wrote what Joseph translated.

The writing was by the great prophet Abraham. Abraham lived in Egypt long ago. Jesus talked with Abraham.

Jesus told Abraham about our life before we came to earth. Jesus said he created the earth. He made the sun, moon, and stars. He made the plants, animals, and people.

Abraham 3—4

Abraham wrote about the gospel of Jesus Christ. The Book of Abraham helps us understand the prophets and the priesthood.

Abraham 1:31

The Writings of Joseph Smith

The third part of the Pearl of Great Price was written by Joseph Smith. In Joseph Smith—History, Joseph told about his first vision. He told how he got the gold plates. Joseph also told how angels from heaven gave him and Oliver Cowdery the priesthood. In Joseph Smith—Matthew, Joseph corrected part of the Bible.

The fourth part of the Pearl of Great Price is the Articles of Faith. One day a man came to see Joseph Smith. The man was writing a book. He wanted something about the Church in his book. He asked Joseph Smith to tell how the Church began.

Joseph Smith wrote about the beginning of the Church. He told what the people in the Church believe. God helped Joseph Smith know what to write. Joseph wrote thirteen important things. He called them the Articles of Faith.

On 1 March 1842, the Articles of Faith were printed in the Church newspaper. The Saints read the Articles of Faith. They believed what Joseph had written.

THE ARTICLES OF FAITH

We believe in God, the Eternal Father, and in His Son, Jesus Christ, and in the Holy Ghost.

We believe that men will be punished for their own sins, and not for Adam's transgression.

We believe that through the Atonement of Christ, all mankind may be saved, by obedience to the laws and ordinances of the Gospel.

We believe that the first principles and ordinances of the Gospel are: first, Faith in the Lord Jesus Christ; second, Repentance; third, Baptism by immersion for the remission of sins; fourth, Laying on of hands for the gift of the Holy Ghost.

We believe that a man must be called of God, by prophecy, and by the laying on of hands by those who are in authority, to preach the Gospel and administer in the ordinances thereof.

We believe in the same organization that existed in the Primitive Church, namely, apostles, prophets, pastors, teachers, evangelists, and so forth.

We believe in the gift of tongues, prophecy, revelation, visions, healing, interpretation of tongues, and so forth.

We believe the Bible to be the word of God as far as it is translated correctly; we also believe the Book of Mormon to be the word of God.

We believe all that God has revealed, all that He does now reveal, and we believe that He will yet reveal many great and important things pertaining to the Kingdom of God.

We believe in the literal gathering of Israel and in the restoration of the Ten Tribes; that Zion (the New Jerusalem) will be built upon the American continent; that Christ will reign personally upon the earth; and, that the earth will be renewed and receive its paradisiacal glory.

We claim the privilege of worshiping Almighty God according to the dictates of our own conscience, and allow all men the same privilege, let them worship how, where, or what they may.

We believe in being subject to kings, presidents, rulers, and magistrates, in obeying, honoring, and sustaining the law.

We believe in being honest, true, chaste, benevolent, virtuous, and in doing good to all men; indeed, we may say that we follow the admonition of Paul—We believe all things, we hope all things, we have endured many things, and hope to be able to endure all things. If there is anything virtuous, lovely, or of good report or praiseworthy, we seek after these things.

Joseph Smith

The Kirtland Temple Is Dedicated

Chapter 39 (January–March 1836)

The Lord had commanded the Saints to build a temple in Kirtland. The Saints worked very hard to build the Kirtland Temple. They finished some of the rooms.

Then the Saints had the first meeting in the temple. At the meeting Joseph Smith's father blessed the leaders of the Church. Joseph's father was the Patriarch of the Church.

Then Joseph had a wonderful vision. He saw the celestial kingdom of heaven. The celestial kingdom is where God lives. Joseph saw how beautiful the celestial kingdom is. He saw Heavenly Father and Jesus. Joseph saw his brother, Alvin, who had died.

D&C 137:1–5

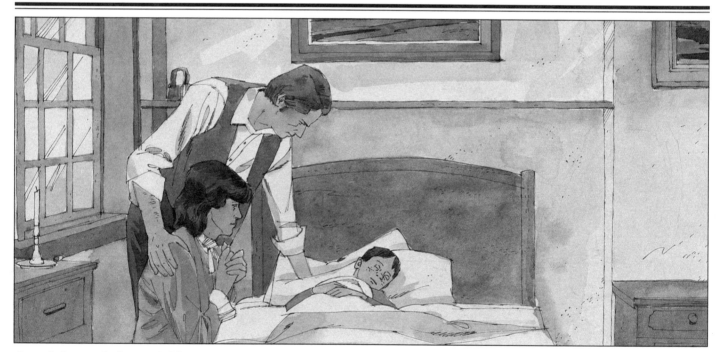

Joseph learned about children who die before they are eight years old. Jesus said they will go to the celestial kingdom.

D&C 137:10

Jesus said many people did not know about the gospel when they lived on earth.

D&C 137:7–9

Other people will live on earth and will not learn about the gospel.

D&C 137:7–9

Some of these people would believe the gospel if they knew about it.
These people can go to the celestial kingdom.

D&C 137:7–9

At last the Kirtland Temple was finished. It was time for the temple to be dedicated. That means the temple would be given to the Lord. It would be used only for the Lord's work. The Saints had a special meeting to dedicate the temple.

Many Saints came to the meeting. They were very happy to have the temple. The Saints sang and prayed to Heavenly Father. They promised to do what the Prophet and other leaders told them to do.

Joseph Smith read a prayer to dedicate the temple. Then the temple was a sacred building. It was the house of the Lord. Angels were in the Kirtland Temple that day. The Holy Ghost was there with the Saints. It was a wonderful day.

D&C 109

Visions in the Kirtland Temple

Chapter 40 (April 1836)

One Sunday afternoon, the Saints had a meeting in the Kirtland Temple. The Apostles blessed the sacrament. Joseph Smith and his counselors passed the sacrament to the Saints.

D&C 110: Preface

Then Joseph Smith and Oliver Cowdery went to a place by themselves in the temple. They knelt down and prayed. After their prayer, a wonderful thing happened. They saw the Lord Jesus Christ. His eyes were bright, like fire. His hair was as white as snow. His face was brighter than the sun.

D&C 110: Preface, 1–3

Jesus told Joseph and Oliver many wonderful things. He said he was
their Savior. He had died for them. He had been resurrected. Jesus said
the people who built the temple should be very happy. Jesus said he
was pleased with the temple. It was his holy house. Jesus said he would
come to the temple many times. He would talk to the Saints. But if the
Saints did not keep the temple holy, he would not come.

D&C 110:4–8

Then Joseph and Oliver saw angels in the Kirtland Temple. First they
saw Moses. Moses was a prophet who lived long ago. He led the
Israelites out of Egypt. The story of Moses is in the Old Testament and
the Pearl of Great Price. Moses gave special priesthood power to Joseph
and Oliver. Then they could help the Israelites come together from all
parts of the earth.

D&C 110:11

Next, Joseph and Oliver saw Elias. Elias brought the priesthood power
of Abraham to the Church of Jesus Christ. Abraham lived long ago. God
blessed Abraham. He gave Abraham special priesthood power.
Abraham's family would always have the priesthood. Righteous
members of the Church become part of Abraham's family.

D&C 84:33–34; 110:12; Abraham 2:8–11; Genesis 12:2–3; 13:16

Then Joseph and Oliver saw Elijah. Elijah was a prophet who lived long
ago. Elijah said people should learn about their ancestors. People should
do temple work for their ancestors. Elijah gave special priesthood power
to Joseph and Oliver. The priesthood power helps righteous families.
They can be sealed to each other. Then they can live together forever.

D&C 2:2; 110:13–16; 1 Kings 17–2 Kings 2; Malachi 4:5–6

Trouble in Kirtland

Chapter 41 (1837)

The Saints in Kirtland, Ohio, were happy. The Lord blessed them.

Some elders left Kirtland. They went to teach people the gospel. Many people listened to the elders and joined the Church.

Then trouble started in Kirtland. The Saints had a bank. They put their money in the bank.

Some of the Saints wanted to get a lot of money. One man who worked at the bank was not honest. He stole some money.

Joseph Smith told the other men to take good care of the money. But the men did not obey Joseph. The bank had to be closed. All the money was gone. The Saints could not get their money back.

Many of the Saints were angry. They said it was Joseph Smith's fault the bank closed. Some of Joseph's best friends said bad things about him. Some of them wanted to kill Joseph.

Some of the Church leaders were angry. They did not want to be members of the Church anymore. They became enemies of the Church. They were wicked. Joseph Smith was very sad.

Other Church leaders loved Joseph and helped him. They knew the Church of Jesus Christ was true. Brigham Young was one of the righteous leaders. Brigham told the Saints he knew Joseph was a prophet of God.

The enemies of the Church were angry at Brigham Young. He had to leave Kirtland so they could not hurt him.

The enemies of the Church made much trouble in Kirtland. They went into the temple and did wicked things.

The temple was not sacred anymore. It could not be the House of the Lord. Joseph was sad because the people were doing wicked things. He was sorry there was so much trouble.

Far West, Missouri

Chapter 42 (January–July 1838)

The wicked people in Kirtland would not repent. They wanted to kill Joseph Smith. Joseph had to leave Kirtland. It was winter and very cold. Joseph's enemies followed him. They had knives and guns to kill him.

Joseph had to hide. The Lord protected him so his enemies could not find him. One night Joseph slept in the same house with his enemies. They did not know he was there.

Another time Joseph passed his enemies on the street. They looked at him. They did not know him.

Joseph traveled hundreds of miles. He went to Far West, Missouri. The Saints in Missouri were happy to see him.

Some of the leaders in Missouri were not obeying God's commandments. They would not repent. They were angry at Joseph. They wanted to get rich.

Joseph was sad. These men had been his friends. Oliver Cowdery, David Whitmer, and other people were excommunicated. They were not members of the Church of Jesus Christ anymore.

Other men were chosen to be the leaders of the Church in Far West.

One day Joseph Smith went to a place near Far West. Jesus said this
place was named Adam-ondi-Ahman. It is a special place. Jesus talked
with Adam there and blessed him. Adam blessed his children at
Adam-ondi-Ahman. Some day Jesus and Adam and other righteous
people will meet there again.

D&C 116

Jesus Christ Names His Church

Chapter 43 (April 1838)

Joseph Smith was in Far West, Missouri. One day Jesus gave him an important revelation. Jesus told Joseph the name of the true church.

The true church is named *The Church of Jesus Christ of Latter-day Saints* because Jesus is its leader. The Church is his church. It is the only true church. Latter-day Saints are the Saints who live now. The latter days are the last days before Jesus will come back to the earth. Saints are righteous people who believe in Jesus Christ. They are members of his true church.

D&C 1:30; 115:4

Tithing

Chapter 44 (July 1838)

The Saints were in Far West, Missouri. The Lord had told Joseph Smith his people should pay tithing. Joseph prayed to Heavenly Father. He asked how much tithing the Saints should pay. He had a revelation from the Lord. The Lord said the Saints should pay one tenth of all they had for tithing.

D&C 64:23; 119: Preface

If they earned ten pennies they should give one penny for tithing. If they earned a hundred pennies they should give ten pennies.

The Saints could pay tithing in other ways. The Saints paid tithing on the crops they grew. They gave one tenth of their grain and hay. They gave one tenth of their chickens and other animals. They paid tithing on milk and vegetables.

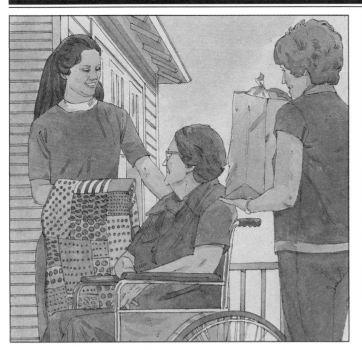

Tithing money is used to help members of the Church. Tithing helps buy food and clothes for needy people.

Tithing is used to build temples and to help missionary work. It is also used to help people who give all their time to work for the Lord.

We give our tithing to the bishop. The bishop gives it to the Church leaders. They decide how to use the tithing.

D&C 120

Heavenly Father gives wonderful blessings to Saints who pay tithing. Saints who do not pay tithing cannot have all these blessings. The Bible says Saints who do not pay tithing are robbing God.

Malachi 3:8–10

The Mobs in Missouri

Chapter 45 (1833)

Some of the Saints were living in Far West, Missouri. Joseph Smith lived there. The people were happy. They built good homes and schools.

But the Saints did not have peace very long. Wicked people made trouble for them. They told lies about the Saints. They said bad things about the Church leaders.

A mob met to plan ways to hurt the Saints.

The mob did many wicked things. They chased the Saints out of their homes.

They burned their homes and destroyed their farms.

They beat the men and put some of them in jail.

The mobs hurt the women and killed some of them.

Mr. Boggs was the governor of Missouri. The mob told him lies about the Saints.

Governor Boggs told some soldiers to kill the Saints if they did not leave Missouri. The mob was glad. They did many other wicked things. The governor did not stop them.

Some Saints lived in a town named Haun's Mill. One day some of them were working in the fields. Others were working in their homes. A mob came and attacked them.

Some of the Saints ran into a building made of logs. The mob shot through the cracks in the walls.

The mob killed the Saints who were hiding. Some children were shot and killed.

Then the mob robbed the homes and wagons of the Saints. They killed many of the men. The women and children were alone.

Later some soldiers captured Joseph Smith and other Church leaders. The soldiers were told to shoot Joseph and his friends.

But the leader of the soldiers would not obey. He would not shoot Joseph and the others. He said it would be murder.

The soldiers put Joseph and his friends in jail. The guards put chains on them. It was cold in the jail. Joseph and his friends had to sleep on the cold floor.

The guards were wicked men. They swore and told bad stories. They told how they robbed and killed the Saints. They told how they hurt the women and children. They laughed and bragged all night.

Joseph hated what they were saying. He did not want to hear any more. He stood up and commanded them in the name of Jesus Christ to stop. He said, "Stop! Or you or I will die this instant." The guards were afraid. They told Joseph they were sorry. They sat in a corner and were quiet.

Brigham Young was one of the Apostles. He asked the Saints to come to a meeting while Joseph was in jail. Brigham Young told them they must leave Missouri. Many of the Saints were poor. They did not have wagons or horses. The men at the meeting said they would help the poor Saints move.

The Saints left Missouri. It was winter and very cold. The mob tried to hurt them. The mob stole the Saints' horses and cows.

The Saints went to Quincy, Illinois. People in Quincy were kind to them.

Governor Boggs and his friends were glad the Saints had gone. The only Saints left in Missouri were in jail.

Joseph Smith in Liberty Jail

Chapter 46 (March 1839)

Joseph Smith and his friends were in jail for many days. Then they were taken to another jail. It was in Liberty, Missouri.

The Liberty Jail was cold and dirty. Joseph and his friends suffered very much. Sometimes they were tied with chains. They had to sleep on the floor.

The food was not good. Sometimes it was poisoned and made them sick.

Joseph was sad. He and his friends had been in jail a long time. Joseph did not know if they would ever get out. He was worried about the Church.

Joseph prayed to Heavenly Father. He asked how long he and the Saints must suffer. He asked Heavenly Father to help them. Joseph asked Heavenly Father to punish their enemies.

D&C 121:1–6

Jesus told Joseph he would only have to suffer a little while. He told Joseph to be brave. Then God would bless him. Jesus said Joseph would soon be with his friends. Joseph's friends loved him and would be happy to see him.

D&C 122:7–9

Jesus knew what the wicked people had done. He told Joseph how he would punish them. The wicked people could never have the priesthood. Their children could never have the priesthood. The wicked people would suffer and die.

D&C 121:15, 21

Jesus told Joseph many good things would happen to the Saints. Nothing could stop God from blessing them. The Holy Ghost would tell them wonderful things about the power of God. They would learn about heaven and earth.

D&C 121:26–33

Jesus said Joseph should not be afraid when he had to suffer. Joseph should not worry when he had troubles. Jesus said troubles are for our own good. Troubles help us learn. Jesus had suffered more than anyone.

D&C 122:7–9

Joseph Smith Asks the President for Help

Chapter 47 (March–November 1839)

Joseph Smith wrote letters to the Saints while he was in Liberty Jail. He told them to write about the wicked things the mobs had done to them. They should send what they had written to the leaders of the country.

D&C 123:1, 4, 6

Joseph told the Saints to write the names of the wicked people who hurt them. They should tell how their homes and farms were destroyed.

D&C 123:1–3

One day some guards were taking Joseph and his four friends to another jail. Joseph and his friends bought two horses from the guards. They gave them clothing to pay for one horse. They promised to pay for the other horse later.

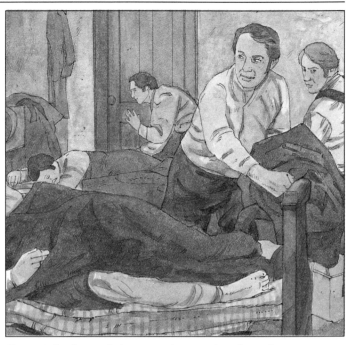

One night four of the guards got drunk and went to bed. Another guard helped Joseph and his friends escape.

Joseph and his friends took turns riding the horses. They went to Quincy, Illinois. It took them ten days to get there.

Joseph and his friends found their families. They were happy to be with them again.

The Saints wanted to find a place in Illinois to build a city. They bought
some land by the Mississippi River. The land was wet and muddy.
Joseph and the Saints moved there. They worked hard to make the land
dry. They built homes and planted gardens. They built a beautiful city.
They named the city Nauvoo. Nauvoo means a beautiful place.

Later, Joseph Smith went to see the president of the United States. Joseph told the president about the mobs in Missouri. He told how the wicked people had burned the Saints' homes and stolen their animals.

Joseph said some of the Saints were killed. Other Saints were put in jail. He showed the president what the Saints wrote. Joseph said the leaders in Missouri would not help the Saints. He asked the president to help the Saints and punish their enemies.

The president said he knew the Saints suffered. But he would not do anything to help them. If he helped the Saints, the people in Missouri would be angry.

Joseph was sad because the president would not help the Saints. Only Heavenly Father would help them.

Missionaries in Other Lands

Chapter 48 (June 1837–October 1841)

The Lord wanted people in other lands to learn about the gospel. He told Joseph Smith some of the Saints should go on missions to England. Elder Heber C. Kimball and three other men were chosen to go. They sailed to England on a ship.

They met a man who was a leader of another church. The man let the missionaries preach in his church. Many of the people believed the missionaries. They wanted to be baptized. This made the leader angry. He said the missionaries could not preach in his church any more.

The missionaries preached in the homes of the people. Many of the people joined The Church of Jesus Christ of Latter-day Saints.

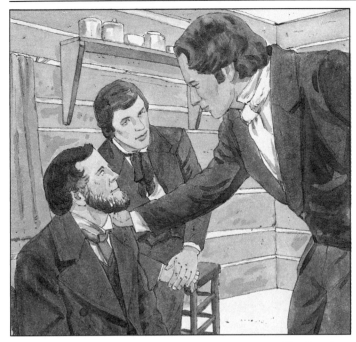

Later other men were going on missions to England. Some of them were Apostles. Joseph talked to them before they went. He told them what they should teach the people.

Joseph told the Apostles to obey all of God's commandments. He talked to them about the priesthood. He said only the true Church of Jesus Christ has the priesthood.

The men were ready to go on their missions. They did not have any money. Many of them were sick. Some of their wives and children were sick. But the men knew Heavenly Father would help them and would bless their families.

The missionaries went to England. They preached in many towns. Thousands of good people believed the gospel. They joined the Church of Jesus Christ. Heavenly Father blessed the missionaries. They all came home safely after their missions.

Orson Hyde was one of the Twelve Apostles. Joseph Smith said Orson had special work to do for the Jews. Orson went to the land of Palestine. On October 24, 1841, he said a prayer to dedicate the land of Palestine.

He asked Heavenly Father to bless the land. He prayed that there would be water so crops could grow. He prayed that all the children of Abraham could go to Palestine to live. They could build homes and gardens there.

God has blessed the land of Palestine. Now it is called Israel. In 1979, President Spencer W. Kimball said a prayer to dedicate a garden in Israel. It is called The Orson Hyde Memorial Garden.

The Saints in Nauvoo

Chapter 49 (January–July 1841)

Joseph Smith and many Saints were living in Nauvoo, Illinois. Jesus gave Joseph some important revelations. Jesus said he was happy with the work Joseph had done. Jesus said all the kings and leaders in the world should be told about the gospel.

D&C 124:1–8

Jesus said the Saints should build a temple in Nauvoo. He wanted the Saints to give gold and silver for the temple. They should bring many kinds of beautiful wood to build the temple.

D&C 124:26–27

Jesus said he would come to the temple. He would give revelations about his church and priesthood.

D&C 124:27, 40

Jesus told Joseph the Saints needed to be baptized for people who had died. He said they should build a baptismal font in the temple. They could be baptized for the dead in the font.

D&C 124:29–37

Jesus said he loved Joseph's brother, Hyrum. Hyrum Smith would be the Patriarch of the Church. He would give special blessings to the Saints.

D&C 124:91–92

One day, the Lord gave Joseph a revelation about Brigham Young. Jesus said he loved Brigham Young. He knew Brigham had worked hard for the Church. He had been away from home on many missions. He had left his family many times.

D&C 126:1–2

The Lord said Brigham Young should stay with his family. He should take special care of them.

D&C 126:3

The First Endowments

Chapter 50 (May 1842)

Jesus promised Joseph Smith that He would give the people a special blessing. This blessing is called an endowment. The endowment would be given in the temple. Only men and women who obey God's commandments could have the endowment.

D&C 105:12, 18, 33; 110:9; 124:40–41

Later, Joseph Smith had a meeting with some of the men and their wives. Joseph taught them the things they would do in the temple. Then endowments were given to all of them.

Now people who obey God's commandments can go to the temple. They can have the special blessing of the endowment. They learn things they need to know to go back to heaven. They make covenants with God. God makes covenants with them.

The Relief Society

Chapter 51 (March 1842)

The members of the Church were building the Nauvoo temple. The men's clothes were wearing out. The women wanted to help them. One woman said she would make clothes for the men. But she did not have money to buy cloth.

Sarah M. Kimball said she would give the women some cloth. Sister Kimball asked other women to help. The women had a meeting in Sister Kimball's home. They decided to have a society for women in the Church.

The women asked Eliza R. Snow to write some rules for the society. She took the rules to Joseph Smith. Joseph Smith said the rules were very good. But he said the Lord had a better plan for the women.

Joseph Smith asked the women to come to a meeting on 17 March
1842. He said the priesthood leaders would help the women with their
society. There were eighteen women at the meeting. Emma Smith was
chosen to be the leader of the women. They called their society the
Relief Society.

Joseph Smith told the women to help people who were sick or poor. They should give people any help they needed. The bishop would help the women know what to do.

The women had meetings to learn the things they should know. They were very glad they could help the members of the Church.

The women made things for the temple. They made clothes for the men who were building the temple.

The women took food to people who needed it. They took care of people who were sick. They did many things to help the Saints.

Women in the Church can go to Relief Society. They help people. They learn about the gospel. They learn about people in other lands. They learn about good books, music, and art. They learn how to make their homes better.

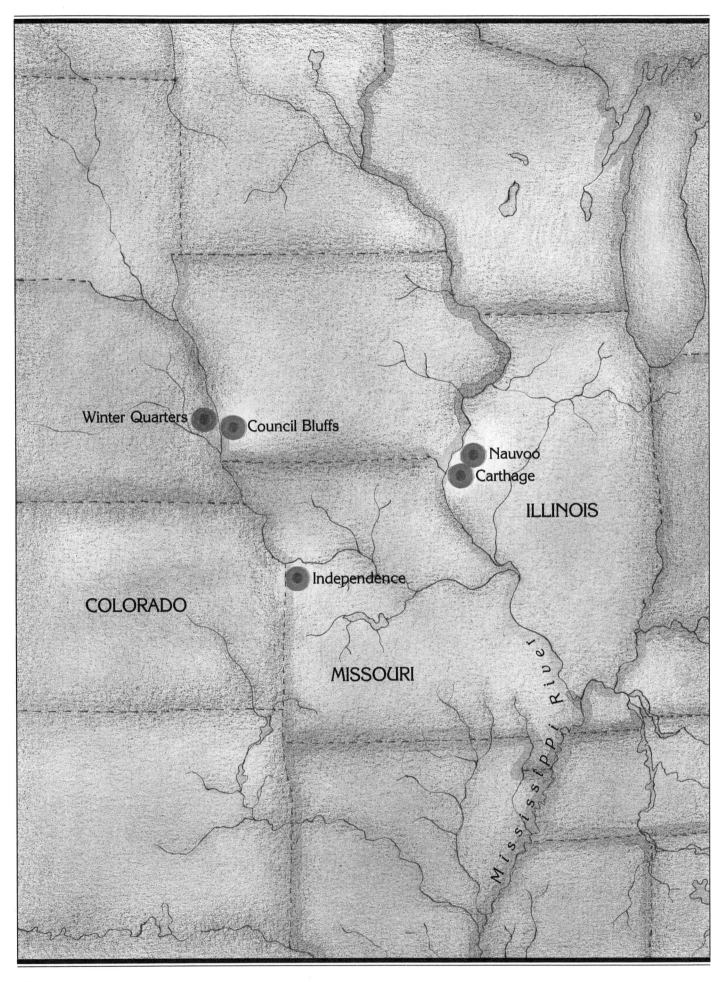

Winter Quarters

Council Bluffs

Nauvoo

Carthage

ILLINOIS

COLORADO

Independence

MISSOURI

Mississippi River

Trouble in Nauvoo

Chapter 52 (May–August 1842)

Many people went to live in Nauvoo. They built a beautiful city. They started to build the temple. The Saints in Nauvoo wanted a mayor for the City.

The Saints chose John C. Bennett to be the mayor of Nauvoo. At first he was a good mayor. But he began to do wicked things. He did not like Joseph Smith.

The people in Nauvoo wanted to have a special holiday. They wanted the soldiers to march in a parade.

John Bennett was a leader of the soldiers. He decided the soldiers would have a battle. It would not be a real battle. It would only be for fun.

Mr. Bennett asked Joseph Smith to lead the soldiers in the battle. Joseph Smith knew that John Bennett did not like him. He thought Mr. Bennett wanted to kill him. The Lord told Joseph he should not be in the battle.

John Bennett was angry. He did not want to be the mayor of Nauvoo anymore. The people chose Joseph Smith to be the mayor.

John Bennett and some other men did not want to be members of the Church. They said bad things about the Prophet Joseph Smith.

Joseph Smith talked to some men who were members of the Church.
He said the Saints would have more trouble. Some day they would have
to leave Nauvoo. They would go to the Rocky Mountains. The Saints
would build cities there. They would obey God and become a strong
people.

God and Angels

Chapter 53 (February–April 1843)

One day a man came to see Joseph Smith. The man said he saw an angel. He told Joseph Smith how the angel was dressed. Joseph Smith said the man was wrong. He said angels do not dress the way the man said.

The man was very angry. He commanded fire to come down from heaven to burn the Prophet and his house. But the man did not have the power of God. No fire came down from heaven.

Jesus gave Joseph Smith a revelation about angels. Jesus said angels
are people who lived on earth. They died and were resurrected. They
have bodies of flesh and bones. Now they live with God.

D&C 129:1

Jesus said Satan tries to trick people. Sometimes he makes people think
he is an angel. He tries to get the people to do wicked things. But
righteous people are able to know when Satan is trying to trick them.

D&C 129:8

Later, Joseph Smith told the people other things about heaven. People who were righteous on earth will live in heaven with Jesus Christ. In heaven they will know everything they learned on earth.

D&C 130:6, 7

Joseph Smith said all God's laws were made in heaven before we came to earth. There is a blessing for each law. We must obey the law to have the blessing.

D&C 130:20–21

Joseph Smith told the Saints about Jesus Christ and Heavenly Father. Jesus looks like a man. He lived on earth. He died and was resurrected. He has a body of flesh and bones.

D&C 130:22

Heavenly Father has a body of flesh and bones. He lives in a beautiful, shining place.

D&C 130:7, 22; Abraham 3:4

Joseph Smith also said the Holy Ghost is a spirit. The Holy Ghost does not have a body of flesh and bones.

D&C 130:22

A Revelation about Marriage

Chapter 54 (July 1843)

Joseph Smith asked the Lord some questions about marriage. Jesus told him that a man and woman should be married by a man who has the priesthood. They should be married in the temple. They should obey God's commandments. Then they will be married forever.

D&C 132:1–29

Righteous people who are married forever will live in the celestial kingdom of heaven. Their children who obey God will belong to them. They will be a family. They will live with God. They will become like him.

D&C 132:1–29

Jesus said sometimes God tells his prophets that men should have more than one wife. But men should do this only when God commands them.

D&C 132:32–39

More Trouble for the Saints

Chapter 55 (1843–1844)

Most of the people near Nauvoo were not members of the Church. Many of them did not like the Saints. They did not want the Saints to be leaders of the city. They made trouble for the members of the Church.

Those people gathered together in mobs. They stole the Saints' animals. They burned barns and houses. They tried to get the Saints to leave Nauvoo. The police and the soldiers would not stop the mobs. The governor would not help the Saints.

Joseph Smith had told the Saints in Nauvoo they would have trouble. The things Joseph Smith had said came true. Joseph knew the Saints would have to leave Nauvoo. They should go to a place where no one would bother them.

Joseph Smith had a meeting with the Apostles and some other men. He told them to find a place where the Saints could go to live.

Joseph Smith looked at maps of the land. The maps showed a place where there were tall mountains and wide valleys. Indians lived there. Joseph knew this would be a good place for the Saints. The mobs could not hurt them. Joseph hoped the Saints could go there to live.

Other people in Nauvoo had been members of the Church. But they did not believe the gospel anymore. They hated Joseph Smith. They wanted to kill him. They started a newspaper. They wrote bad things about Joseph and the Saints.

The leaders of Nauvoo were angry about the newspaper. Some of them went to the newspaper building. They burned the newspapers. They destroyed the printing press. The newspaper could not be printed anymore.

The Prophet Is Killed

Chapter 56 (June 1844)

Some people blamed Joseph Smith for the trouble in Nauvoo. Joseph was put in jail. The judge said Joseph Smith had done nothing wrong. He let Joseph go.

The mobs were very angry with the judge. They said they would kill the judge. The Saints in Nauvoo were afraid. They asked the governor of the state to help them. But he would not. He sent soldiers to find Joseph Smith.

Joseph Smith knew he might be put in jail again. Joseph was afraid his brother Hyrum would also be put in jail. Joseph told Hyrum to take Hyrum's family and go to another city. But Hyrum would not leave Joseph.

Joseph Smith said he and Hyrum should leave Nauvoo. If they did the mobs would not hurt the Saints. So Joseph and Hyrum went across the river.

Some people said Joseph Smith was running away because he was afraid. Joseph's wife, Emma, sent some friends to ask him to come back. Joseph Smith thought he would be killed if he went to Nauvoo. But he did what his friends wanted him to do.

Joseph and Hyrum went back to Nauvoo. They were arrested. The soldiers took them and Willard Richards and John Taylor to a town named Carthage. They put them in the Carthage Jail.

The next day was 27 June 1844. Some of Joseph Smith's friends visited him in the jail. They read the scriptures. John Taylor sang one of Joseph's favorite songs about Jesus.

Suddenly they heard a noise outside. A mob was shooting at the jail.
There were more than one hundred men in the mob. They painted their
faces so no one would know who they were.

Some of the mob ran past the guard and pushed open the door of the
jail. They ran upstairs. They shot into the room. They shot John Taylor,
but they didn't kill him. They killed Hyrum. Joseph saw that Hyrum was
dead. He said, "Oh, dear brother Hyrum!"

Joseph Smith ran to the window. The mob shot him. He cried, "O Lord, my God." He fell out the window. The prophet of God was dead.

The bodies of Joseph Smith and his brother Hyrum were taken to Nauvoo. The Saints were very sad. Their leader and prophet was dead. He gave his life for the gospel of Jesus Christ.

D&C 135

The Prophet Joseph Smith did much important work. He translated the
Book of Mormon. He started the true Church of Jesus Christ. He sent
missionaries to teach the gospel in other lands. He built a city where the
Saints could live. God loved Joseph Smith. The Saints loved him.
Joseph Smith did more to help us than any other man, except Jesus
Christ.

D&C 135:3

A New Leader for the Church

Chapter 57 (July–August 1844)

The Prophet Joseph Smith was dead. The Church did not have a President. The Saints did not know who should be their leader.

Most of the Apostles were far away on missions.

Sidney Rigdon had been Joseph Smith's counselor. But he had not obeyed the Lord. He had moved away from Nauvoo.

D&C 124:108–109

Sidney Rigdon heard the Prophet was dead. He came back to Nauvoo. He wanted to be the leader of the Church.

Brigham Young and the other Apostles came back from their missions. Brigham Young was the leader of the Apostles. He said the Apostles should lead the Church until a new President was chosen.

D&C 107:24

The members of the Church had a meeting. Sidney Rigdon spoke to them. He said he should be the leader of the Church.

Then Brigham Young spoke. He said the Apostles should lead the
Church. The Holy Ghost was with him. Brigham Young's voice sounded
like Joseph Smith's voice. For a few minutes, he looked like Joseph
Smith. The people knew that God had chosen the Apostles to lead the
Church. Sidney Rigdon was angry. He went back to his home. He started
a church of his own. He was not a member of The Church of Jesus
Christ of Latter-day Saints anymore.

The First Saints Leave Nauvoo

Chapter 58 (September 1845–February 1846)

After Joseph Smith was killed the mobs thought the Church would end. They did not know the Lord would choose a new leader. The mobs wanted to destroy the Church. The newspapers told lies about the Saints. They said the Saints were killing people and stealing.

The Governor of the state would not help the Saints. He said the mobs hated them. He told the Saints to move to the West. Brigham Young said the Saints would go West. But they needed time to get ready. They needed money to buy food and clothes. They had to make wagons and buy oxen. They must sell their houses.

The mob did not want to give the Saints time to get ready. The people would not buy the Saints' homes. The mob made some of the Saints leave their homes. They stole things from the houses. Then they burned the houses.

The Saints worked hard to get ready to leave Nauvoo. They cut wood and made wagons. They bought animals. They gathered food. The Saints wanted to finish the temple before they left.

The Saints gave money to build the temple. They worked on the temple. They finished many of the rooms. They dedicated each room when it was finished. They used one room to baptize people for the dead. They had a conference in the temple for all the Church members.

Winter came. It was very cold. The mobs made many Saints leave their homes. The Saints put all their things in their wagons. They drove the wagons on to flat boats. They went across the Mississippi river.

It was so cold the river froze. Brigham Young and some of the Saints drove their wagons across the river on the ice.

The Saints camped by the river. Some of the people did not have enough clothes. They were very cold. Some of them did not have enough food. Saints who had enough food and clothes shared with others. The Saints stayed by the river for a few days. Then they moved and made another camp. Brigham Young chose leaders. The leaders helped the people get ready to travel to the mountains in the West.

The Nauvoo Temple Is Finished

Chapter 59 (October 1845–September 1846)

Some of the Saints did not leave Nauvoo. The Lord had told the Saints to build a temple in Nauvoo. They wanted to obey him. The people who stayed in Nauvoo worked hard on the temple.

D&C 124:31

Many of the Saints were sick. Most of them were poor. They knew they must leave Nauvoo soon. But they still wanted to finish the temple.

At last the temple was finished. The Saints did temple work all day and all night. They were given their endowment. They were very happy to have the temple.

At last the rest of the Saints had to leave Nauvoo. They put all their things in their wagons. They crossed the Mississippi River to the other side.

They looked back across the river and saw Nauvoo. They saw the temple on the hill. They were sad to leave Nauvoo. But they were glad they had finished the temple of the Lord.

The Saints stayed by the river for a few days. They did not have enough food to eat. The Lord helped them. He sent some small birds called quail. The Saints killed the quail and ate them.

Then Brigham Young sent some men to help the Saints. The men took them to the place where the other Saints were camped.

The Pioneers Travel On

Chapter 60 (March 1846–June 1846)

Early in the spring the Saints began to travel again. It was still very cold. Some of the people got sick and died.

The roads were very bad. The people had to travel slowly. The land was flat with a few small hills. The land was covered with tall grass. This kind of land is called a plain. Indians lived on the plains. There were no cities or farms.

Brigham Young sent men to find good places for the people to camp.
They cut trees and made log houses. They built bridges across streams.
They made it easier for the people to travel. The Saints who were
traveling to the West were called pioneers.

The pioneers came to a wide river. The place where they stopped was
called Council Bluffs. Other Saints came to join them. They built camps
nearby. The pioneers stayed there until summer.

The Mormon Battalion

Chapter 61 (June 1846–July 1847)

The Saints were at Council Bluffs. A captain of the United States Army came to see Brigham Young. His name was Captain Allen.

Captain Allen said the president of the United States wanted 500 men to join the army. Brigham Young said the Saints would do what the president wanted.

Captain Allen talked to the men and 500 of them joined the army. They were called the Mormon Battalion. Sometimes members of the Church are called Mormons because they believe in the Book of Mormon.

Brigham Young told the men to be the best soldiers in the army. They should take the Bible and Book of Mormon with them. They must be neat, clean, and polite. They should not swear or play cards. Brigham Young told the men to obey God's commandments. Then they would not have to kill anyone.

The Mormon Battalion went with Captain Allen. The Saints were sad to see them go. The Saints needed all the men to help them go West. They did not want the men to go away to fight. But they knew the soldiers would be paid. The money would help the Saints.

The Mormon Battalion traveled south. Some of the families of the soldiers were with the Mormon Battalion. It was very hard for the people to travel. They had to walk all the way.

The roads were very bad. Sometimes the wagons got stuck in the deep sand. There was no water to drink. There were no trees where the men could rest in the shade. Some people got sick. Only the sick people could ride in the wagons.

Captain Allen decided the sick soldiers and the women and children should stay in Colorado. They stayed at a town called Pueblo. The soldiers were paid for being in the army. Some of the sick soldiers sent money to their families in Council Bluffs. They sent money for the poor people in Nauvoo and for the missionaries.

The soldiers in the Battalion kept marching. Sometimes they did not know where they were going. They had to dig down into the sand to find water. The water tasted bad. The soldiers did not have enough food. There was no wood to make fires. The men had to burn weeds.

The soldiers met Indians and other people who had food. The soldiers did not have money to buy food. They gave the Indians some of their clothes. The Indians gave the soldiers some food.

The Mormon Battalion traveled west. They came to some very steep
mountains. The men had to tie ropes on the wagons and pull them up
the mountains. Then they let the wagons down the other side.

One day the soldiers saw some bulls. The bulls attacked the soldiers.
The soldiers fought the bulls. At last they chased the bulls away. One
man was hurt. He could not walk for a long time.

At last the Mormon Battalion came to the Pacific Ocean. It was 29 January 1847. The men were very tired. Their clothes were ragged. They were glad their long march had ended.

The soldiers were paid for being in the army. They did not have to be in the army anymore. They could go home to their families.

Some of the men stayed in California. Most of them went to the Rocky Mountains to be with the other Saints who had arrived there from Council Bluffs.

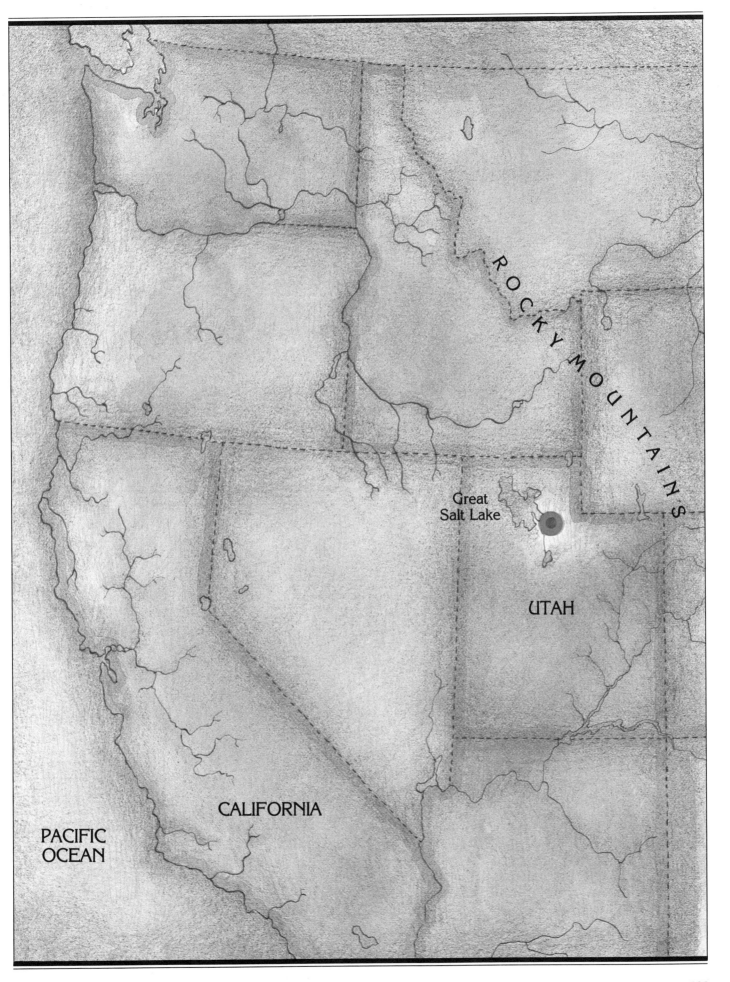

Great
Salt Lake

ROCKY MOUNTAINS

UTAH

CALIFORNIA

PACIFIC
OCEAN

223

The Pioneers Go to Salt Lake Valley

Chapter 62 (June 1846–July 1847)

The pioneers were still at Council Bluffs. They needed many strong men to help them travel. Most of the young men were with the Mormon Battalion. So the pioneers decided not to go to the Rocky Mountains until spring.

The Indians let the Saints have some land on the other side of the river. There the Saints built a town named Winter Quarters. They made streets and built houses. Some houses were made of logs. Other homes were in caves in the side of the hills. The pioneers planted crops.

Brigham Young divided the city into wards. He chose men to be bishops. Some Indians made trouble for the pioneers. The pioneers built a wall around the city to keep out the Indians who made trouble.

While the pioneers were in Winter Quarters Brigham Young had a revelation. The Lord told him how the people should get ready to leave. He told Brigham Young what the people should do as they traveled.

The Lord said the people should be divided into small groups. Each group would have a leader. The people should obey their leaders. They should help each other. They should take care of families that had no mother or father.

D&C 136:1–8

Each group should have its own wagons and food. Each group should have people who knew how to fix the wagons, build houses, plant crops, and build bridges.

D&C 136:7

The Lord told the Saints other things they should do. They should keep his commandments. They should keep their promises to each other. They should not say bad things about each other. They should be honest. They should give back things they borrowed or found.

D&C 136:23–27

The Lord wanted the pioneers to be happy. He told them to sing and dance together. They should not be afraid. He would help them. He told them they would have troubles. But their troubles would make them better people. They would be blessed.

D&C 136:28–31

Brigham Young did what the Lord told him to do. He divided the people into groups. Each group had everything they would need to build a city in the mountains.

The Saints had a conference. Then Brigham Young chose a group to leave first. There were 143 men, three women, and two children. The next day the first group left Winter Quarters.

Everyone had a job to do on the way. The women took care of the children. They cooked the food. The men all had guns to protect the people and animals.

The pioneers traveled all day. At night they camped. They put their wagons in a circle. The people and animals stayed inside the circle. They built fires and cooked their food.

They danced and sang. One of the songs was "Come, Come, Ye Saints." It made the people feel better.

A man blew a bugle to tell them it was time to go to bed. The pioneers said their prayers and went to sleep.

The pioneers traveled a long way across the plains. They traveled for four months. They met other people on the way. Some of the people were trappers. They told Brigham Young not to go to the Rocky Mountains. They said crops would not grow there.

Other people told Brigham Young to take the Saints to California. But Brigham Young said the Lord had shown him where the Saints should go. He would obey the Lord.

At last the pioneers came to the mountains. It was hard to travel there.

Brigham Young got sick. He could not travel very fast. He chose some men to go ahead. He told them to go to the Great Salt Lake Valley. They should begin to plant crops.

The men took their wagons over the mountains. They went down into the valley. They camped by a stream.

They prayed to the Lord. They asked him to bless the seeds they were going to plant. The men planted the seeds.

The next day Brigham Young and the pioneers with him came to the valley. Brigham Young looked at the valley from his wagon. He knew it was the place where the Lord wanted the Saints to live. Brigham Young said, "This is the right place. Drive on." The Saints drove their wagons down into the valley. It was 24 July 1847.

The Saints in the Rocky Mountains

Chapter 63 (July 1847)

The pioneers began to build a city in Great Salt Lake Valley. They named the city Salt Lake City. Brigham Young chose a place to build the temple.

Brigham Young divided the city. Each family had some land for a house and a farm. The pioneers built log houses. They planted crops. They worked hard. Brigham Young taught the Saints that everyone must work for what he needed.

Brigham Young divided the city into five wards. The people began to build churches. More pioneers came to the valley. Soon there were nineteen wards.

The pioneers started a school. School classes and church meetings were in the same building. Later the Sunday School was started.

Brigham Young sent missionaries to other lands across the ocean. In some places only a few people joined the Church.

In other places many people believed the missionaries. They joined the Church. Many of them wanted to live with the Saints in Great Salt Lake Valley. They crossed the ocean in ships.

Some of the people crossed the plains in covered wagons. But some
people did not have money to buy wagons. They made small carts with
two wheels. They were called handcarts. The pioneers put all their things
in the carts. They pushed and pulled the carts across the plains. It was
very hard work to push the carts. Some of the people got sick and died.

Brigham Young was a wise leader. He sent men and their families to other places in the West. Some Saints built towns in California. Other Saints built towns in Idaho, Arizona, and Wyoming. Some of the people were sorry to leave their homes. But they obeyed Brigham Young.

The Saints had many troubles. Sometimes their crops would not grow. Floods washed away their farms. Sometimes Indians stole things from the Saints or killed them.

Brigham Young told the Saints to be kind to the Indians. The Saints gave food to the Indians. Many of the Indians became friends of the Saints.

The Saints began to build temples in the West. In 1853 they started to build the temple in Salt Lake City. They worked forty years to build the temple. The Saints built three other temples before the Salt Lake temple was finished. They built the St. George Temple, the Logan Temple, and the Manti Temple.

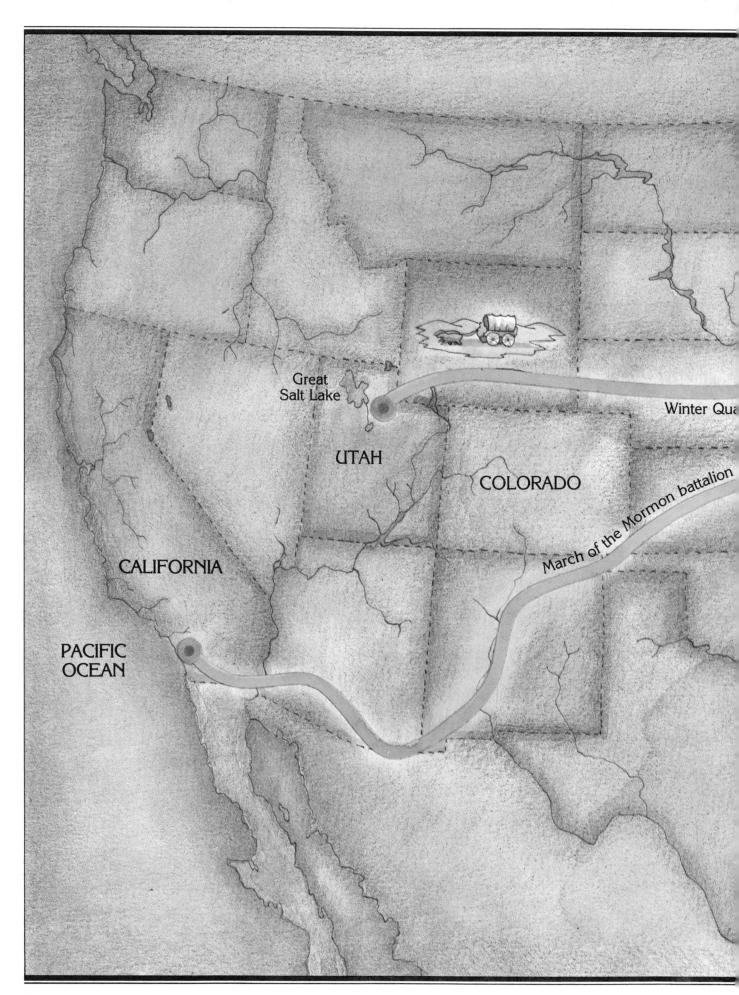

Great
Salt Lake

UTAH

COLORADO

Winter Qua

March of the Mormon battalion

CALIFORNIA

PACIFIC
OCEAN

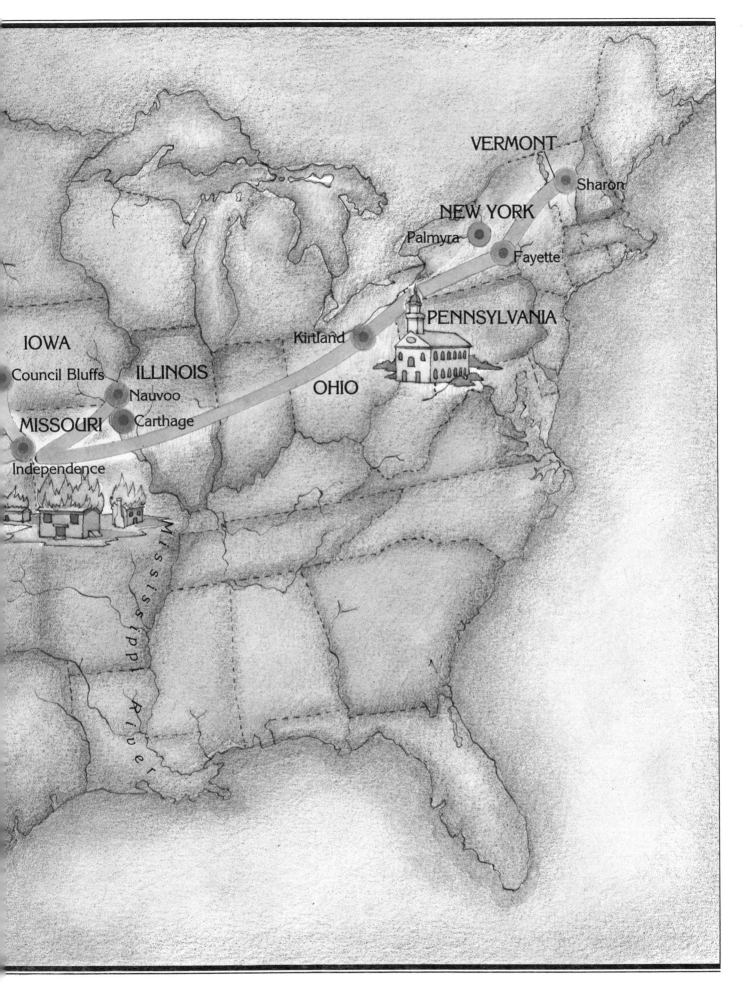

VERMONT

Sharon

NEW YORK

Palmyra

Fayette

PENNSYLVANIA

IOWA

Council Bluffs

ILLINOIS

Nauvoo

Kirtland

OHIO

MISSOURI

Carthage

Independence

Mississippi River

The Church of Jesus Christ Today

Chapter 64

Many years have gone by since the Church was started in Fayette, New York. The Church had grown much bigger in those years. In 1830, six people started the Church, while others watched.

Missionaries went to many lands to teach the gospel. People listened to the missionaries. They believed the gospel and joined the Church. In 1983, there are more than four million members of the Church. The people are very different. They live all over the world. They speak many languages. They are happy to be members of the Church.

On 6 April 1980, the Church had a birthday. It was 150 years old. The Church had a special conference on its birthday. There were two meetings at the same time. One meeting was in Fayette, New York. The prophet Spencer W. Kimball was there in a house just like Peter Whitmer's home.

The other meeting was in the tabernacle in Salt Lake City. There were thousands of people at the meeting. President Kimball talked to the Saints on television. He dedicated the Peter Whitmer house. All the members of the Church were very happy to see and hear the prophet. Members of the Church are very blessed. We should be grateful that we are members of The Church of Jesus Christ of Latter-day Saints. We have a prophet to lead us.

Words to Know

Adopted Joseph and Emma Smith <u>adopted</u> twin babies.
Joseph and Emma <u>made</u> the twin babies <u>part of their family</u>.
alcohol Beer and wine have <u>alcohol</u> in them.
<u>Alcohol</u> is not good for us to drink.
ancestors Our <u>ancestors</u> are the people in our family who lived before us.

angel An <u>angel</u> is one of God's helpers.
The <u>angel</u> Moroni talked to Joseph Smith.
Apostle An <u>Apostle</u> is a leader in the Church of Jesus Christ.
Jesus told Joseph Smith he wanted 12 <u>Apostles</u>.
arrested The soldiers <u>arrested</u> Joseph Smith.
The soldiers caught Joseph Smith and put him in jail.
attacked The mob <u>attacked</u> the Saints.
The mob began to fight the Saints.
baptismal font There are <u>baptismal fonts</u> in churches and temples.
People are baptized in a <u>baptismal font</u>.
baptized When we join the Church we are <u>baptized</u>.
We are put down under the water and brought up again.

beautiful When something is <u>beautiful</u> we like to look at it.
A garden is <u>beautiful</u>.
The temple is <u>beautiful</u>.
believe To <u>believe</u> means to think something is true.
Many people <u>believe</u> the gospel of Jesus Christ.
bishop A <u>bishop</u> is a leader in the Church.
The leader of a ward is the <u>bishop</u>.
blamed The people <u>blamed</u> Joseph Smith for the trouble.
The people said Joseph Smith made the trouble happen.
borrow When we <u>borrow</u> something we ask someone if we can use it.
borrowed The man <u>borrowed</u> his friend's horse.
The man asked his friend if he could use his horse.
bragged The guards in the jail <u>bragged</u> about what they had done.
They were happy about it.
bridge The pioneers crossed the river on a <u>bridge</u>.

bugle A <u>bugle</u> is a kind of horn.
building The temple is a large <u>building</u>.
built The pioneers <u>built</u> their houses of logs.
buried Moroni <u>buried</u> the gold plates.
He put the plates in a hole in the ground.
He covered them with dirt.
captain A <u>captain</u> is a leader.
Captain Allen was the leader of the soldiers.
captured The solders <u>captured</u> Joseph Smith.
The soldiers caught Joseph Smith and would not let him go.
choices Heavenly Father lets us make <u>choices</u>.
Heavenly Father lets us decide what we will do.
choked The men <u>choked</u> Joseph Smith.

choose God lets us choose to be good or bad.
We choose people to be leaders.
God chose Brigham Young to lead the Saints.

commandments Good people obey God's commandments.
Good people do what God wants them to do.

conference A conference is a large meeting.
Many members of the Church go to conference.

counselors Counselors are people who help a leader.
The prophet of the Church has counselors.

covenant A covenant is a promise.
We promise God that we will do something.
We make a covenant with God.

created Jesus Christ created the earth.
Jesus Christ made the earth.

crops The pioneers planted crops.
The pioneers planted corn, potatoes, wheat, and other things.

crossed The pioneers crossed the river.
The pioneers went to the other side of the river.

crucified Jesus was crucified.
Jesus was killed. He was nailed on a cross and hung there until he died.

dam The Saints built a dam in the river.
A dam holds back the water.

deacons Boys may be deacons when they are 12 years old.
Deacons may pass the sacrament.

decided Emma and Joseph wondered whether to go to Pennsylvania or to stay in New York. They decided to go to Pennsylvania.

dedicate When we dedicate something we bless it to be used for God's work.
The Saints dedicated the temple.

destroy To destroy means to tear down, break, burn, or kill.
The mobs destroyed the temple.

disciple A disciple is a person who follows Jesus and tries to be like him.

divided The leader divided the land.
The leader gave a part of the land to each family.

earn To earn means to get something by working for it.
The men worked for the farmer.
They earned some money.

elders Elders are men who have the priesthood.

endowment An endowment is a special promise or gift from God.

enemy An enemy is a person who hates another person.
Joseph Smith's enemies tried to kill him.

escape To escape means to get away from someone or something.
The men tried to escape from the jail.
Joseph Smith escaped from the mob.

evil Evil is something very bad.
Satan is an evil spirit.

evil spirits Evil spirits are bad spirits.
Evil spirits follow Satan.

excommunicated Members of the Church who do wicked things can be excommunicated.
They cannot be members of the Church.

faith To have faith is to know something is true.
We have faith in Jesus Christ.
We believe in him and obey him.

fast To fast is to go without food or water.
The people fasted for three days.
The people did not eat or drink anything for three days.

forever Forever means always.
We can live with Heavenly Father forever if we obey his commandments.

forgive To forgive means to forget the bad things someone has done.
God will forgive us if we are sorry for the bad things we have done and never do them again.

gather To gather means to come together in one place.
Joseph Smith told the Saints to gather in Missouri.

gifts Gifts are things that are given to people.
The Holy Ghost gives gifts to people who are righteous.

gospel The gospel is what Jesus teaches us to do.
The Saints believe the gospel of Jesus Christ.

governor A governor is the leader of a state.

guards The guards watched the men in the jail so they could not get away.

heal To heal means to make sick people well.
Newel Whitney blessed Joseph Smith.
Joseph Smith was healed.

honest People who are honest do not tell lies.
Honest people do not take things that do not belong to them.

jail The men were put in jail.
The men were locked up so they could not get away.

joined The people joined the Church.
The people were baptized and became members of the Church.

kingdom The kingdom of heaven is where God lives.

language The words we use to write or talk to other people are called languages.

lead To lead people means to show or tell them what to do.
The prophet leads the Church.

leader The prophet is the leader of the Church.

marriage Marriage is being married.

married Joseph and Emma were married.
Joseph was Emma's husband.
Emma was Joseph's wife.

members The people were members of the Church.
The people were baptized and belonged to the Church.

mission The Apostle went on a mission.
The Apostle went to tell people about the gospel of Jesus Christ.

missionary A missionary is a person who goes on a mission.

mountain The pioneers drove their wagon up the mountain.

obey To obey means to do what we are told to do.
We should obey God's commandments.

ocean An ocean is a lot of water with land around it.

240

ordained To be ordained means to be given the priesthood.
Joseph Smith ordained the man.
Joseph Smith gave the man the priesthood.

oxen Oxen are animals.
patriarch A patriarch gives special blessings to people.
Joseph Smith's father was a patriarch.
poison Poison is something that can kill people if they eat or drink it.
The mob tried to make Joseph Smith drink poison.
pray To pray means to talk to Heavenly Father.
Joseph Smith prayed to Heavenly Father.
Joseph Smith talked to Heavenly Father.
prayers The pioneers said their prayers and went to bed.
The pioneers prayed and went to bed.
preached Joseph Smith preached to the people.
Joseph Smith talked to the people and told them about the gospel.
presidency The presidency of the Church is the president and his counselors.
president A president is a leader.
The president of the Church is the leader.
priesthood The priesthood is the power of God.
priests Priests have the priesthood.
Priests are men who help in the Church.
printed The words in this book are printed on paper.
printer A printer is a man who prints books.

prison A prison is a place where people are put and cannot get out.
A prison is like a jail.
prophet A prophet tells the people what God wants them to know.
Joseph Smith was a prophet.
protect The men had guns to protect the people.
The men had guns to keep the people safe.
The Lord protected Joseph Smith.
The Lord kept Joseph Smith safe.

quails Quails are birds.
repent If we do something bad we should repent.
If we do something bad we should feel sorry and not do it any more.
resurrected Jesus Christ was resurrected.
He had been dead. He is alive again.
All people will be resurrected after they die.
righteous Righteous people do what is right.
They obey God's commandments.
Sabbath The Sabbath is the day we go to Church.
We should not work on the Sabbath.
Sunday is the Sabbath day.

sacrament We take the sacrament to remember Jesus.
We take the bread and water to remember Jesus.

sacred The temple is a sacred building.
The temple belongs to God.
Saint A member of the Church of Jesus Christ.
save Jesus died to save us.
Jesus died so we could go back to live with Heavenly Father.
scriptures The scriptures are books that tell us about God.
The Bible, Book of Mormon, the Doctrine and Covenants, and the Pearl of Great Price are scriptures of the Church.
share To share means to give part of what we have to someone.
soldiers Soldiers fight in an army.
spirit A spirit does not have a body of flesh and bones.
steal To steal means to take something that is not yours.
Mobs stole the Saints' animals.
The mobs took the animals.
suffer We suffer when our bodies hurt.
Joseph Smith and his friends suffered in jail.
swear To swear means to say bad words.
swore The guards in the jail swore.
The guards in the jail said bad words.
tar Tar is sticky and black.
temple A temple is the house of God.
tempt Satan tried to tempt us.
Satan tried to get us to do things that are bad.
tithing Tithing is the money we give to God.
tobacco Some people smoke and chew tobacco.
Tobacco is not good for us.
translated Joseph Smith translated the Book of Mormon.
Joseph Smith wrote the Book of Mormon in words we know.
trouble Trouble is something bad that happens to us.
The Saints in Nauvoo had many troubles.
truth Jesus teaches people the truth.
Jesus teaches people what is right.

testimony A testimony is a feeling that the gospel is true.
The man had a testimony that the gospel is true.
trappers Trappers are people who catch wild animals.
They sell the animals' fur.
vision A vision is something that God lets us see.
Joseph Smith saw Heavenly Father and Jesus Christ in a vision.
wicked The man did wicked things.
The man did things that were bad.
witnesses The witnesses saw the gold plates.
They said that the gold plates were real.
worship To worship means to love and obey.
Satan wanted Moses to worship him.
Satan wanted Moses to love and obey him.
wound A place where someone's body has been hurt or cut.

Places to Know

Adam-ondi-Ahman   Adam-ondi-Ahman is in the state of Missouri. Jesus visited Adam there long ago.

America   America is the land where the Book of Mormon people lived long ago.

Arizona   Arizona is in the western part of the United States. Brigham Young sent Saints to build towns in Arizona.

California   California is in the western part of the United States. Brigham Young sent Saints to build towns in California.

Carthage   Carthage is a town in the state of Illinois. Joseph and Hyrum Smith were killed in the Carthage Jail.

celestial kingdom of heaven   The celestial kingdom of heaven is where Heavenly Father and Jesus live. Righteous Saints will live there after they are resurrected.

Colorado   Colorado is a state in the western part of the United States.

Council Bluffs   Council Bluffs was a town on the plains of the United States.

earth   The earth is the place where we live now. Jesus Christ made the earth.

Egypt   Egypt is a land where Abraham and Moses lived long ago.

Far West   Far West was a town in the state of Missouri. The Saints lived in Far West for a while.

Fayette   Fayette is a town in the state of New York. Joseph Smith started the Church in Fayette.

Garden of Gethsemane   The Garden of Gethsemane is near Jerusalem. Jesus suffered and bled for us in the Garden of Gethsemane.

Great Salt Lake Valley   The Great Salt Lake Valley is in the western part of the United States.

Harmony   A town in Pennsylvania where Joseph Smith lived.

Haun's Mill   Haun's Mill was a town in the state of Missouri. A mob killed many Saints in Haun's Mill.

heaven   Heaven is the place where Heavenly Father and Jesus live. We lived in heaven before we came to earth.

Hill Cumorah   The Hill Cumorah was near Joseph Smith's home in the state of New York. The gold plates were buried in the Hill Cumorah.

Idaho   Idaho is in the western part of the United States. Brigham Young sent Saints to build towns in Idaho.

Illinois   Illinois is a state in the United States. Nauvoo and Carthage are towns in Illinois.

Independence   Independence is a city in Jackson County, Missouri. Jesus said the city of Zion would be built near Independence.

Israel   Israel is a land where many of the Jews live.

Jackson County   Jackson County is in the state of Missouri. The mobs made the Saints leave Jackson County.

Jerusalem   Jerusalem is a city in Israel. Jesus will go to Jerusalem when he comes back to the earth.

Kirtland   Kirtland is a town in the state of Ohio. The Saints built a temple in Kirtland.

Liberty   Liberty is a town in Missouri. Joseph Smith was in the Liberty Jail.

Mississippi River   The Mississippi River is near the city of Nauvoo. The Saints crossed the Mississippi River when they left Nauvoo.

Missouri   Missouri is a state in the United States. Independence is a city in Missouri.

Nauvoo   Nauvoo is a city in the state of Illinois. The Saints lived in Nauvoo and built a temple there.

New York   New York is a state in the United States. The Hill Cumorah is in New York. Fayette is in New York.

Ohio   Ohio is a state in the United States. Kirtland is a town in Ohio.

Pacific Ocean   The Pacific Ocean is on the western side of the United States. The Mormon Battalion marched to the Pacific Ocean.

Palestine   Palestine is the land where the Israelites lived.

Palmyra   The town in New York where Joseph Smith grew up.

Pennsylvania   Pennsylvania is a state in the United States. Emma Smith's family lived in Pennsylvania.

Pueblo   Pueblo is a city in the state of Colorado. The men in the Mormon Battalion left their families in Pueblo.

Quincy Quincy is a town in the state of Illinois.

Rocky Mountains The Rocky Mountains are in the western part of the United States. The pioneers crossed the Rocky Mountains and went into the Great Salt Lake Valley.

Salt Lake City The pioneers built Salt Lake City. It is in the Great Salt Lake Valley.

telestial kingdom of heaven People who are not good on earth will live in the telestial kingdom of heaven after they are resurrected.

terrestrial kingdom of heaven People who are good but do not obey all God's commandments on earth will live in the terrestrial kingdom of heaven after they are resurrected.

United States The United States is a land in North America. The Church of Jesus Christ of Latter-day Saints was started in the United States.

Utah Utah is a state in the United States. Salt Lake City is in Utah.

Vermont Vermont is a state in the United States. Joseph Smith was born in Vermont.

Winter Quarters Winter Quarters was a town on the plains of the United States.

Wyoming Wyoming is in the western part of the United States. Brigham Young sent Saints to build towns in Wyoming.

Zion Zion was a city that Enoch built. Some day there will be another city named Zion. It will be in Jackson County, Missouri.

People to Know

Abraham   Abraham was a prophet who lived long ago. The story of Abraham is in the Old Testament and the Pearl of Great Price.

Bennett, John C.   John C. Bennett was a mayor of Nauvoo. He did not like Joseph Smith.

Brother Allen   A Church member who was tarred and feathered in Missouri.

Captain Allen   Captain Allen was a captain in the United States Army. He asked the men of the Church to be in the Mormon Battalion.

Copely, Leman   A Church member in Kirtland, Ohio, who wouldn't share his land with other members.

Cowdery, Oliver   Oliver Cowdery helped Joseph Smith translate the gold plates. He did much work to help the Church of Jesus Christ.

Elias   Elias gave special priesthood power to Joseph Smith and Oliver Cowdery in the Kirtland Temple.

Elijah   Elijah was a prophet who lived long ago. He gave special priesthood power to Joseph Smith and Oliver Cowdery in the Kirtland Temple.

Enoch   Enoch was a prophet who lived long ago. He built the city of Zion. The story of Enoch is in the Pearl of Great Price.

God   Heavenly Father, Jesus Christ, and the Holy Ghost are all Gods. They all have great power.

Governor Boggs   Governor Boggs was the governor of Missouri. He would not help the Saints.

Harris, Martin   Martin Harris helped Joseph Smith translate the gold plates. He lost some pages of the Book of Mormon.

Heavenly Father   Heavenly Father is the father of our spirit bodies. We pray to Heavenly Father. Sometimes we call our Heavenly Father God.

Holy Ghost   The Holy Ghost has a spirit body. He helps Heavenly Father and Jesus. He has power to give the Saints special gifts. He helps them know what is right.

Hyde, Orson   Orson Hyde was an Apostle. He dedicated the land of Palestine for the children of Abraham to have a place to live.

Indians   Indians lived in all parts of the United States. Sometimes Indians are called Lamanites.

Israelites   Israelites were people who lived in Palestine long ago.

James   James was one of Jesus' Twelve Apostles. Peter, James, and John gave the Melchizedek Priesthood to Joseph Smith and Oliver Cowdery.

Jesus Christ   Jesus Christ is our Savior. He is the Son of Heavenly Father. Sometimes we call Jesus the Lord.

John   John was one of Jesus' Twelve Apostles. Peter, James, and John gave the Melchizedek Priesthood to Joseph Smith and Oliver Cowdery.

John the Baptist   John the Baptist lived when Jesus lived on the earth. John the Baptist gave the Aaronic Priesthood to Joseph Smith and Oliver Cowdery.

Kimball, Heber C.   Heber C. Kimball was an Apostle. He went on a mission to England.

Kimball, Spencer W.   Spencer W. Kimball is the 12th president of the Church. He is an Apostle and a prophet.

Knight, Newel   Newel Knight became sick when Satan tried to stop him from praying. Joseph Smith healed Newel Knight.

Lamanites   Indians are called Lamanites in the Book of Mormon.

Lord   Sometimes we call Jesus Christ the Lord.

Melchizedek   Melchizedek was a prophet who lived long ago. He had the priesthood.

Mormons   Sometimes members of the Church are called Mormons because they believe the Book of Mormon.

Moroni   Moroni was a prophet who lived in America long ago. He buried the gold plates in the Hill Cumorah.

Moses   Moses was a prophet who lived long ago. He led the Israelites out of Egypt. He gave special priesthood power to Joseph Smith and Oliver Cowdery in the Kirtland Temple.

Mr. Chandler   Mr. Chandler sold some rolls of old paper to the Saints in Kirtland. The writings of

Abraham were on the rolls of paper.

Mr. Hale Mr. Hale was Emma Smith's father.

Noah Noah was a prophet who lived long ago. Noah had the priesthood.

Page, Hiram Hiram Page said he had a stone that gave him revelations for the Church.

Partridge, Edward Edward Partridge was the first bishop of the Church.

Peter Peter was one of Jesus' Twelve Apostles. Peter, James, and John gave the Melchizedek Priesthood to Joseph Smith and Oliver Cowdery.

Phelps, William W. William W. Phelps helped start schools in Jackson County, Missouri.

Pioneers The pioneers were the Saints who went across the plains to the Rocky Mountains.

Pratt, Parley P. Parley P. Pratt went on a mission to teach the Lamanites.

Richards, Willard Willard Richards was a friend of Joseph Smith. He was with Joseph in Carthage Jail.

Rigdon, Sidney Sidney Rigdon was one of Joseph's counselors.

Satan Satan is the devil. Satan wants to stop Heavenly Father's work on the earth. He wants to destroy the Church of Jesus Christ.

Sister Vilate Kimball Sister Kimball was Heber C. Kimball's wife. She was a member of the first Relief Society.

Smith, Alvin Alvin Smith was Joseph Smith's older brother. He died. Joseph saw a vision of Alvin in the celestial kingdom of heaven.

Smith, Emma Emma Smith was Joseph Smith's wife. She was the first leader of the Relief Society. She made a song book for the Church.

Smith, Hyrum Hyrum Smith was Joseph Smith's older brother. Hyrum was killed in the Carthage Jail with Joseph.

Smith, Joseph Joseph Smith was the first prophet and president of The Church of Jesus Christ of Latter-day Saints. Jesus gave Joseph Smith the revelations that are in the Doctrine and Covenants. Joseph was killed in the Carthage Jail.

Smith, Joseph Sr. Joseph Smith, Sr. , was Joseph Smith's father.

Smith, Lucy Lucy Smith was Joseph Smith's mother.

Smith, Samuel Samuel Smith was Joseph Smith's younger brother. He was the first missionary for the Church.

Snow, Eliza R. Eliza R. Snow was a member of the first Relief Society.

Taylor, John John Taylor was a friend of Joseph Smith. He was with Joseph in Carthage Jail. Later he became President of the Church.

Whitmer, David David Whitmer was a witness who saw the gold plates. He helped start the Church on 6 April 1830.

Whitmer, Peter Peter Whitmer helped start the Church on 6 April 1830.

Whitney, Newell Newel Whitney was the second bishop of the Church.

Williams, Frederick G. Frederick G. Williams was one of Joseph Smith's counselors.

Young, Brigham Brigham Young was one of the Twelve Apostles. He was the leader of the pioneers. He was the prophet of the Church after Joseph Smith.

Young, Phineas Phineas Young was Brigham Young's brother.

The Hill Cumorah

The Sacred Grove

The Susquehanna River (photo by Jed A. Clark)

The Kirtland Temple

"Entering Nauvoo," by C. C. A. Christensen (BYU Art Museum Collection)

A Home in Nauvoo

In Nauvoo (photo by Jed A. Clark)

The Brigham Young Home, Nauvoo

The Orson Hyde Home, Nauvoo (photo by Jed A. Clark)

The Carthage Jail, Carthage, Illinois

The Salt Lake Temple and Church Headquarters, Salt Lake City

Joseph Smith, 1830 - 1844

Brigham Young, 1847 - 1877

John Taylor, 1880 - 1887

Wilford Woodruff, 1889 - 1898

Lorenzo Snow, 1898 - 1901

Joseph F. Smith, 1901 - 1918

Heber J. Grant, 1918 - 1945

George Albert Smith, 1945 - 1951

David O. McKay, 1951 - 1970

Joseph Fielding Smith, 1970 - 1972

Harold B. Lee, 1972 - 1973

Spencer W. Kimball, 1973 -